Horizon

SUMMER, 1967 · VOLUME IX, NUMBER 3

The Smugglers' Trail

Our lead story in this issue begins, like any good Oriental mystery, with a chance encounter between a foreign traveler and a dark-eyed lady on a train speeding through the Turkish night. The traveler is allowed to feast his eyes on a fabulous treasure. Then the lady and the treasure both disappear.

The traveler in this tale is James Mellaart, a British archaeologist who has twice written for HORIZON about his discoveries in Anatolia. The treasure that the lady laid before him was the Treasure of Dorak, dug from the site of an ancient civilization close to Troy. Its trail leads us, as it led Mellaart, into the murky underworld of international smuggling.

Turkey, whose oldest settlements are just coming to light, is the scene of the greatest archaeological looting job since Lord Elgin made off with the sculptures of the Parthenon. Because the Turkish government forbids the export of any ancient art objects, whatever comes out of that country must be smuggled out. And the smugglers' trail, which begins in remote Anatolian villages, leads in the end, as often as not, to some of the world's most famous museums.

European museums like the Louvre (which is stuffed to the eaves with the booty of Napoleon's campaigns) and the British Museum (which houses the Elgin Marbles) acknowledge their recent Turkish acquisitions with a sophistication born of long experience. But American curators seem more sensitive about their role as buyers of smuggled property. When HORIZON requested information and photographs of Turkish objects at the Metropolitan Museum in New York and Dumbarton Oaks in Washington, D.C., the officials of those institutions reacted like children caught with their hands in the cookie jar.

Countries that include ancient sites have generally adopted one of two policies to control the trade in antiquities. One—the policy of Greece and Italy as well as Turkey—is to forbid all export. The other is to take any "unique treasure" for the government and divide the rest, half and half, with the discoverer. This is the policy of Egypt, Iran, and Iraq, and it goes far to explain why foreign museums prefer to finance digs in those countries.

The important lesson for the Turks to learn

HORIZON is published every three months by American Heritage Publishing Co., Inc.

PRESIDENT
James Parton

EDITORIAL COMMITTEE
Joseph J. Thorndike, *Chairman*
Oliver Jensen
Richard M. Ketchum

SENIOR ART DIRECTOR
Irwin Glusker

SENIOR EDITOR, HORIZON
Marshall B. Davidson

PUBLISHER, HORIZON
Paul Gottlieb

Editorial and executive offices:
551 Fifth Avenue, New York, N.Y. 10017.

EDITOR
Joseph J. Thorndike

MANAGING EDITOR: Charles L. Mee, Jr.

ARTICLES EDITOR: Robert Cowley   ART EDITOR: Jane Wilson

ART DIRECTOR: Kenneth Munowitz

ASSOCIATE EDITORS: Shirley Tomkievicz, Barbara Klaw

CONTRIBUTING EDITOR: Walter Karp

ASSISTANT EDITOR: Alice D. Watson   EDITORIAL ASSISTANT: Charles Folds

COPY EDITOR: Mary Ann Pfeiffer   *Assistant:* Carol R. Angell

ADVISORY BOARD: Gilbert Highet, *Chairman*, Frederick Burkhardt, William Harlan Hale, John Walker

EUROPEAN CONSULTING EDITOR: J. H. Plumb, *Christ's College, Cambridge*

EUROPEAN BUREAU: Gertrudis Feliu, *Chief, 11 rue du Bouloi, Paris 1er*

HORIZON

A Magazine of the Arts

SUMMER, 1967 · VOLUME IX, NUMBER 3

is that neither policy works unless it is enforced. Italy, for instance, maintains a special force of *polizia archeologica* to wage a never-ending war with the *tomboroli*, or tomb robbers, of Tuscany. As long as a country is a virtual sieve, like Turkey, the world's museums cannot really be censured for buying pieces that would otherwise end up in private collections.

The museums argue that the treasures of ancient art, which naturally abound in the homelands of ancient civilizations, should be spread around the world so that art lovers and students in the "have-not" countries can see the originals instead of plaster copies. Up to a point there is merit in this plea, but it is getting easier all the time to look at ancient art in the lands of its origin. Certainly the argument should not be used to justify the pillage of unique treasures that were designed, as the Elgin Marbles were, to stand in one special place. To claim that these unique pieces should remain in London so that more people can see them is preposterous in an age when a million tourists climb the Acropolis every year. Of course the pots and statues found in Turkey are not, like the Elgin Marbles, parts of a larger monument, but they still have power to evoke a lost civilization. That power is greatest if they are left in the land of their creation.

J.J.T.

All correspondence about subscriptions should be addressed to: HORIZON Subscription Office, 379 West Center St., Marion, Ohio 43302.

　　Single Copies: $ 5.00
　　Subscriptions: $16.00 per year in the U.S. & Canada; elsewhere, $17.00

Annual indexes for Volumes I–VIII are available at $1 each. A cumulative index for Volumes I–V is available at $3. HORIZON is also indexed in the *Readers Guide to Periodical Literature*.

The editors welcome contributions but can assume no responsibility for unsolicited material.

　　　Title registered U.S. Patent Office

Second-class postage paid at New York, N.Y., and at additional mailing offices.

COVER: This pottery vessel, in the shape of a double-headed female, is a handsome example of the art of Stone Age Turkey. It was found at Hacilar, in southwest Turkey, and it is probably more than seven thousand years old. Hacilar art has but recently come to the notice of collectors, and so eager are they to own it that it makes its way—handed from peasant to dealer to smuggler to dealer—all over the Western world. This vase is now in the Ashmolean Museum at Oxford. An article about smuggled Turkish treasures begins on page 4.

A GODDESS AND HER HANDMAIDENS—IN UNIQUE FIGURINES OF 4500 YEARS AGO.

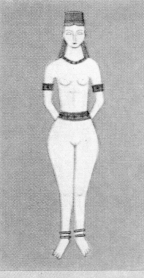

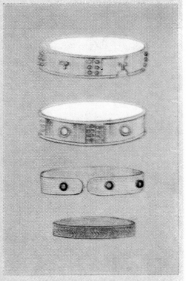

FIG. 3. THE TWO BRONZE FIGURINES—PRIEST-ESSES OR WORSHIPPERS—WEARING WHAT WAS PRESUMABLY THE NORMAL DRESS OF THE YORTAN RULING CLASS (6 INS. HIGH).

FIG. 4. BACK VIEW OF FIG. 3. THE FIGURES ARE OF BRONZE WITH SILVER GARMENTS; AND HAIR, ORNAMENTS AND DECORATION IN GOLD. TWO HAIRSTYLES ARE SHOWN.

FIG. 5. ONE OF THE ATTENDANTS ON THE GODDESS. THE BODY IS ENTIRELY MADE OF SILVER, THE HAIR AND ALL THE ORNAMENTS BEING GOLD.

FIG. 6. PERSONAL JEWELLERY FROM THE QUEEN'S TOMB: GOLD AND SILVER BRACE-LETS, WHOSE PATTERN MAY ALSO BE OBSERVED ON THE FIGURINES.

FIG. 7. THE GODDESS (RIGHT) IN ELECTRUM AND HER PRINCIPAL ATTENDANT IN SILVER, ALL THE ADDITIONAL ORNAMENTS BEING IN GOLD. THE GODDESS'S GOLD BELT AND PENDANTS ARE SOLDERED ON BUT THE "GRASS SKIRT" IS ENGRAVED. LIFE SIZE.

FIG. 8. THE BACK VIEW OF THE TWO FIGURINES SHOWN IN FIG. 9. THE SILVER FIGURE, WEARING A GOLD-EDGED SILVER APRON, HOLDS A CIRCLET, WITH SEVERAL BIRDS ON IT PERHAPS A MUSICAL INSTRUMENT OF THE SISTRUM TYPE.

The Strange Case
of
JAMES MELLAART
—OR—
THE TALE of the MISSING DORAK TREASURE

Is he a thief? A liar? The dupe of an international smuggling ring? Whatever he is, James Mellaart, a HORIZON contributor, has got himself embroiled in the wildest controversy in all the vendetta-racked politics of international archaeology

James Mellaart, discoverer of one of the most important ancient sites in Turkey, stays at home in Istanbul as the site of his dig becomes overgrown. Mellaart's trouble began with his report on the Dorak treasure for the Illustrated London News *in 1959 (see opposite). The bronze, silver, and electrum figurines are the first real evidence (if they exist) of the Yortan culture, which flourished about 3000 B.C.*

The girl who came into the compartment on a Turkish train and sat down opposite James Mellaart was attractive "in a tarty sort of way." He might not have given her a second glance had it not been for the bracelet on her wrist. The average passenger would not have noticed it. Mellaart stared. It was a solid gold bracelet of a type that had been found only at Troy.

Any archaeologist worth his salt would have reacted as Mellaart did. He introduced himself and asked where it had come from. From home, she said. It was part of a collection of antiquities she owned. Mellaart knew that metalwork of this caliber was extremely rare. Curiosity drove the conversation along. Could he see the rest? Yes, the girl agreed.

Thus, on a summer evening in 1958, began the greatest archaeological mystery story of recent times. James Mellaart is a British archaeologist whose spectacular discoveries on the Anatolian plains—twice published in HORIZON*—have since given him a brilliant reputation in his field. In 1958, however, he was a young scholar traveling from his home in Istanbul to Izmir, the trading port of Turkey's Aegean

coast, to look for a place to begin an excavation.

It was dark when the train pulled into Izmir, and the route they took to the girl's house was none too clear. They caught a taxi to the nearest pier, took a ferry across the bay to the district of Karşyaka, and then a second cab to a house in a narrow street. Mellaart was invited to stay to dinner.

Over the meal, in a dining room on the first floor, the archaeologist and the girl, who was speaking English with an American accent, talked nonstop about the collection. This, by now, was being produced bit by bit from a chest of drawers where it lay on cotton wool, covered with dust. Mellaart was doing his best to conceal his excitement; here, it appeared, was something unique in the history of archaeology. Before him lay gold and silver figurines, bracelets, daggers, a delicately wrought drinking cup of pure gold, as well as many other vessels, and even a few textile fragments —the contents of two royal tombs and the first real evidence of a hitherto dimly known culture.

He handled the discussion with great care. One impolitic question might

* "Man's First Murals," September, 1962; "Shapes from the Ancient Earth," November, 1963.

By KENNETH PEARSON *and* PATRICIA CONNOR

easily end the acquaintance. Could he photograph the collection? The girl hesitated. No. That, she suggested, would mean bringing outsiders into the house and letting others know that the treasure existed. But, she added, he could sketch it if he liked.

The collection now on the table included two old, faded photographs of skeletons in two tombs. The pictures were charred at the edges. And there was a series of scientifically compiled notes, some of which also seemed to have been singed. The notes were in modern Greek, which the girl translated. They talked into the early hours of the morning, and Mellaart was invited to stay at the house.

He remained several days, studying the artifacts, drawing their details, making rubbings of the hieroglyphs, and transposing the notes into a lengthy commentary. What Mellaart had in front of him were the results of an excavation made, he was told, during the Greek occupation of Aegean Turkey just after the First World War. The tombs had been discovered near the village of Dorak, south of the Sea of Marmara. They were relics of the Yortan culture, belonging to a neighbor state of Troy, and their date, to judge by an Egyptian import in one of the tombs, was about the middle of the third millennium B.C.

Few Yortan settlements had ever been discovered and none scientifically excavated. And the majority of known graves belonged to villages rather than cities and were never very rich in content. What Mellaart had stumbled across was real evidence of a large seafaring nation, ruled by a warrior aristocracy, immediately east of Troy.

Mellaart worked without a break. He never left the house. If he needed anything, the girl shopped for him. Then late one night Mellaart's work was finished. He left for the station before dawn the next day. The girl promised to see if she could forward photographs of the collection, but in

any case to let him know when he could publish his findings.

Mellaart realized then that in his obsession with the discovery he knew very little about the girl (he had been calling her "Anna") or where he had stayed. "The name is Anna Papastrati," she had told him, "and our address is 217 Kazim Direk Street."

"I never asked any superfluous questions," Mellaart now says. "I was too frightened of putting a foot wrong. I remember I slept in a small room on the first floor. It had a window overlooking a garden at the side. I had a feeling that there was an old man in another room. I thought it might be her father. Because of her accent I assumed she worked for the United States Information Service in Izmir or at the NATO base." Not to have identified the girl beyond this was Mellaart's first mistake.

Back in Ankara, at the British Institute of Archaeology where he was employed as assistant director, Mellaart kept quiet about his find. Archaeologists are reluctant to report discoveries without producing the objects themselves or at least photographic evidence. But no pictures

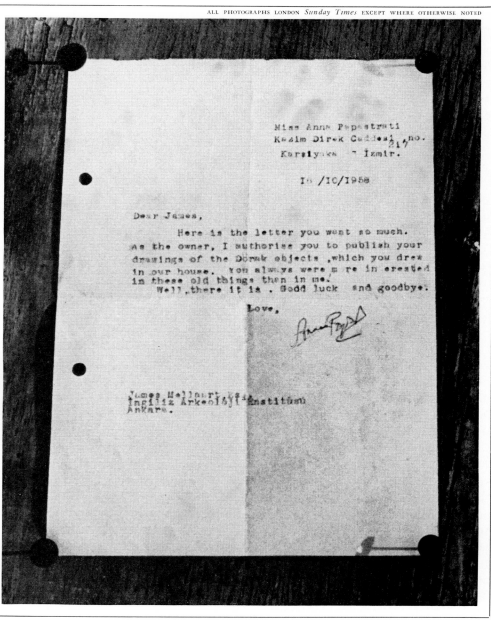

Opposite is the street in Izmir where Mellaart says he stayed with Anna Papastrati. The visit made headlines in the Turkish paper Milliyet *(above) in May of 1962, four years after it occurred.*

Arlette Mellaart (above) has resolutely defended her husband's integrity. The letter at right, written in the style of a ten-cent thriller, is the only proof that Anna—or the treasure—ever existed.

came. A few months later Mellaart revealed to a friend news of the Dorak treasure, and for several days they worked "like excited kids" to tidy up the hasty sketches. Then Mellaart presented his discovery to Professor Seton Lloyd, who was at that time director of the Institute. It was at this point that Mellaart made his second mistake.

He told Seton Lloyd that he had run across the hoard six years earlier and had been asked to keep silent about it. Now permission to publish had been received. "My God, this is dynamite," said Seton Lloyd. "You must report this at once to the Department of Antiquities." Mellaart agreed.

The calculated lie, says the archaeologist, was provoked by personal reasons. At the time of his visit to Izmir, Mellaart had been married for four years, and it hardly seemed expedient to explain to his wife, although he did soon after, that he had just spent several days with a girl. "I knew about it a little later," says Seton Lloyd, "but the man was a fool not to tell me the truth at first."

Twice in the late summer Mellaart wrote to Izmir to ask about the photographs. Neither letter received a reply.

But then on October 10 Anna Papastrati wrote to him.

"Dear James: Here is the letter you want so much. As the owner, I authorize you to publish your drawings of the Dorak objects, which you drew in our house. You always were more interested in these old things than in me! Well, there it is. Good luck and good-bye. Love, Anna Papastrati."

At the time, Mellaart thought this was a reply to his requests for photographs. Now he recognizes that it need not have been. At the same time he admits that its tone could suggest a degree of intimacy between the two

7

that was not obvious at first. "I had to be nice to her," he says. "I wanted to keep in her good books."

Meanwhile Seton Lloyd had taken the sketches to London and was talking over the find with eminent archaeologists, all of whom agreed on the likely authenticity of the treasure and urged publication. This was arranged with the *Illustrated London News.* Seton Lloyd returned to Ankara in March with the good news, and on April 3, Mellaart wrote to the Turkish Department of Antiquities, telling them of forthcoming publication and talking of "a rich collection of metalwork of the Yortan culture" that he had come across.

On November 25, 1959, the *Illustrated London News* carried a four-page spread, handsomely illustrated, on the Mellaart find. The headline was unequivocal: "The Royal Treasure of Dorak—a first and exclusive report of a clandestine excavation which led to the most important discovery since the Royal tombs of Ur."

The news shattered the Turkish authorities. Although an introduction to the article made clear its provenance, and special attention was drawn to the treasure's imaginative reconstruction, there is no doubt that the Department of Antiquities thought a minor "Tutankhamen" had slipped through its hands.

On July 18, 1960, Mellaart went over the details of his trip with the Turkish authorities. Though he included the name of "Anna Papastrati" and her address, investigations in Izmir drew a blank. The Turks could not locate the woman or her house. Kazim Direk Street, they said, was in the commercial center and contained no private homes. (As a matter of fact, Izmir has two such streets, and the Turks were looking at the wrong one.) The Dorak treasure had vanished.

Mellaart's troubles were just beginning, because unfortunately it was only too logical for the Turkish authorities to assume that the treasure

had been taken out of the country, either with the connivance of the archaeologist or without it. Turkey forbids the removal of any work of art from the country. Yet antiquities are being smuggled out in wholesale lots. The art of prehistoric Turkey, much of which Mellaart himself has uncovered, is in great demand among Western museums and collectors. The Hittites, the Trojans, the Greeks, the Romans, the Byzantines—all, in their turn, had flourishing cultures in Asia Minor, and the diversity of Turkey's antique wealth is unparalleled. An increasing number of Turks are angered by the removal of their heritage by outsiders. This is the crux of the Dorak affair.

At first glance, no one seems less likely than Mellaart to be involved in any dishonorable dealings. His colleagues have commented upon his impetuousness and lack of tact, but as the British ambassador to Ankara remarked, "He has a nose for a site that amounts almost to genius." He was in Turkey in the early 1950's, and peasants harvesting in Central Anatolia grew accustomed to seeing his odd figure trudging along the dirt roads. He was then in his mid-twenties, of medium height, and invariably dressed in baggy slacks, a khaki shirt, and sneakers. He carried a rucksack on his back and his pockets were full of stones to chase off prowling sheep dogs. He had arrived on a one-year scholarship of about $1,000, and he made it last two. Even in those days he was being called lucky. It was always said with a twinge of envy. Mellaart had the knack of walking a site for hours, picking a spot to excavate, and striking it rich almost at once.

It isn't luck. He reads signs like a Sherlock Holmes. One day at Jericho a slight depression thrown into relief by the sun low on the horizon led him to rich graves and forty intact vases before breakfast. In Cyprus he once turned down a group outing into town because he could not afford the fare, stayed on the site, and unearthed a

Mycenaean bronze hoard.

He discovered his first important neolithic site at the Turkish village of Hacilar by tracing a trail of local gossip to a nearby coffeehouse; there he found a former chauffeur who produced two significant pots from his house. (Mellaart bought both and presented them to the museum in Ankara.) The trail finally took him to a field on the edge of an orchard where a village dating back to the eighth millennium B.C. lay buried beneath the crops.

Mellaart's Turkish home, an eighteenth-century mansion on the Bosporus near Istanbul, is the house of his Turkish father-in-law, Kadri Cenani, a former executive with Shell in Turkey and now vice-president of the Turkish Press Union. Mellaart's local associations, however, are not the asset they first appear to be. "He's never had to face up to life as 99.9 per cent of the population has," says Charles Burney, an English colleague who also digs in Turkey. "His situation has left him time to devote everything to archaeology and he has become single-minded to a fault."

Mellaart's obsession has its limitations. He surrounds himself with an invisible barrier that only the immediate topic of archaeology can penetrate; then his conversation is inspiring. He is impatient with lesser minds not at once on the same wave length. Mellaart does not argue, he strikes out at people. Lies are always "filthy"; the opinions of those who do not agree with him are usually "stupid."

Mellaart, however, is aware enough of his own limitations to admit all this. As assistant director of the British Institute of Archaeology in Ankara some years ago, he was in line for the directorship. He did not get the job, and it might have proved a disaster if he had. Yet, on this score at least, he shows no bitterness. "I'm useless at administration. All that paper work. It's no good, I don't get on with people. But give me a site and just let me dig. That's all I ever need."

Çatal Hüyük, which James Mellaart discovered in 1958, is the oldest city known to archaeology. By 7000 B.C. its inhabitants were using pottery—in fact they may have invented it. By about 6000 B.C. they were painting frescoes like the one above, on man-made walls—the first people known to have done so. The huge bull is a shrine fresco. The site of Mellaart's excavation now lies deserted. From the tower in the picture below, guards keep watch for illegal diggers.

A villager stands in a hole he has just dug at Hacilar to look for salable works of art. Hacilar was originally Mellaart's excavation, and once he left off, the villagers began. The site has now been bulldozed by the Turkish authorities.

As the Dorak scandal slowly began to gather momentum, Mellaart was doing exactly that. Early in 1961 he began excavations at his greatest site, Çatal Hüyük. The Turks, meanwhile unable to find any trace of Anna Papastrati, handed over their investigation to the Department of Public Prosecutions to see if Mellaart could be brought to trial. Hoping the affair would simply be forgotten, Mellaart stuck to the story he had told and continued with his work.

But on May 29, 1962, two and a half years after the Dorak story had broken in the *Illustrated London News*, Turkey's second leading newspaper, *Milliyet*, launched a three-part attack on Mellaart. On the first day, across all eight columns of the front page, a banner headline exclaimed: "An Historic Royal Treasure Worth a Milliard Lire Smuggled Out." The value of the hoard was estimated at a hundred million dollars.

On the second day, May 30, still in a front-page story, Dorak villagers were quoted as describing "a fair-haired, fat, middle-aged foreigner" seen near the tombs with a woman either in 1955 or 1956. The next day, Mellaart was still page-one news. A photograph showed "a youth of Mustafakemalpasha" (a town near Dorak) who had come forward to identify Mellaart as the man who had been seen. The implication seemed irrefutable: Mellaart had dug up the treasure himself.

Once the Turkish press had the taste of blood, it began to attach Mellaart's name, directly or obliquely, to almost any story that involved the disappearance of antiquities. An official blow against Mellaart was not far away.

On March 3, 1964, the archaeologist, who was at that time in London, received a letter from the Department of Antiquities denying him permission to dig at Çatal Hüyük that season. Mellaart went at once to see the Turkish Ambassador. His Excellency listened attentively to the whole story. "Who's your enemy in Ankara?" he asked. "Find him and you'll know the reason."

At the same time Mellaart's father-in-law intervened. First, he sent a piece of blank paper in a registered letter to the Izmir, Karşyaka district, address; it obliged the post office to account for its travels. It was returned marked: "The addressee was asked for at 217 Kazim Direk Street but the above-named was unknown there." At least Cenani had proved an address existed.

Next he sought help from a former Minister of the Interior. This official gave Cenani a note of introduction to the Chief of Security in Izmir, who put his best man on the job of trying to trace the girl—but without success. The security chief's reaction was significant: "In the absence of any proof to the contrary, Mellaart must be considered faultless. I think the girl was a plant, engineered from Ankara. Somebody knew Mellaart was leaving for Izmir, and the girl was put on his track. If a girl like that had a treasure at home, is it likely that she would pick up anyone on a train, not knowing whether he might denounce her? She knew she was dealing with an archaeologist."

But if the press was pursuing Mellaart relentlessly, how were the authorities in Ankara reacting? There was in fact a slight *détente* in the affair. Diplomatic overtures from the British Institute of Archaeology in the Turkish capital had produced a compromise. The dig at Çatal Hüyük could continue, said the Turks, provided some other English archaeologist was put in charge of the site. Mellaart swallowed his pride. Oliver Gurney, a professor at Oxford, led the 1965 excavations with Mellaart as his assistant. But the arrangement was strictly one of convenience. Gurney went to Turkey for about three weeks, signed all the right papers, and returned to England, leaving Mellaart at home on the site.

The season's dig, archaeologically speaking, was a great success. Çatal Hüyük has emerged as an archaeological site of unique importance—a large neolithic town of about 7000 B.C. with the oldest wall paintings ever found. In his preface to a book Mellaart has written on his findings, Sir Mortimer Wheeler calls the excavation as important today as those at Knossos and Troy were in theirs.

Diplomatically speaking, the 1965 dig was a disaster. The Turks put a guard on the site, and he followed Mellaart like a shadow. Mellaart alleges that the Turks also planted two servants, who spent a great deal of their time reporting back to Ankara.

The result, in view of increasing pressures and the archaeologist's temperament, was inevitable. He blew up. Overnight, his Turkish foreman and three of his workers, men who had been with him for twelve years, took off. And the season petered out in bitter recriminations. Resentment burned deep in Mellaart. His next act was the

Some collectors get their antiquities by dynamiting them out of the ground. Others go discreetly to the Covered Bazaar in Istanbul and whisper "neolithic." With luck they meet a dealer like this one, who has a Hacilar goddess to sell.

ultimate gesture of a man whose emotions blinded reason. In January, 1966, he wrote a letter to the Royal Ontario Museum, one of the many organizations that support him financially. It was addressed to a friend, for publication in the museum's newsletter.

For a start, Mellaart alleged that certain xenophobic elements, aided by the Turkish press and aroused by the Cyprus crisis of 1964, had brought enough pressure to bear to have his digging application refused. He went

on to make bitter allegations of having been spied on by the Turkish authorities. The newsletter fell into the hands of a visiting Turkish archaeologist in New York. Within days the contents had reached Ankara.

On May 11, last year, *Milliyet* carried yet another Mellaart story. This time, it reported, "the General Directorate of Museums is opening an investigation on the archaeologist for the tone of his Ontario letter." The story was filled out with the usual sup-

The Hacilar pot at left was recently bought by the British Museum, the one above by the Louvre. The Dumbarton Oaks Collection in Washington, D.C. (at right) has part of its newly acquired Byzantine silver on display. (The rest of it is in storage awaiting cleaning and restoration.) Officials have declined to allow any photographs to be taken.

positions about the Dorak treasure.

But by this time the British Institute of Archaeology had advised Mellaart not to apply for digging permission at Çatal Hüyük—it would save everyone the embarrassment of a flat refusal. At the site, the weeds grew thicker and longer, and the mud walls dissolved under the winter rain.

Meanwhile, the Turks had not succeeded in collecting enough evidence on the Dorak mystery to put Mellaart on trial. Their police inquiries were inconclusive. On June 6, 1964, just three months after the archaeologist's application for that season had been turned down, the Public Prosecutor wrote to the Minister of Education saying that they had decided to drop the case. New legislation providing amnesty for all foreigners before the courts now merely prolonged the suspense and gave the Turkish press new license to publish its speculations. It has continued to do so till this day.

If Mellaart is not the villain of the piece, as the press insists he is, who is the culprit? To find him—or them—we must look along a smugglers' trail

that begins in villages near the excavations and ends in some of the world's most famous museums. One of the official Turkish complaints is that, once the archaeologists open up a site, the local thieves move in. This is indeed what has happened at another important Mellaart dig at Hacilar; its painted pottery from about 5500 B.C. is now fetching high prices throughout the world—up to $75,000 for a single piece.

On a visit to Hacilar last summer, we had only been there ten minutes when a villager approached us. Were we interested in buying? He had something we might like. A quarter of an hour later, by which time two more villagers had roared up on a motorcycle, he returned with a shoulder bag from which he took an exquisite pot in the shape of a goddess. It could be ours for $560.

But he was small fry. The newest apartment block in the town of Burdur, fifteen miles away, was built on the proceeds of the sale of Hacilar objects. This was stated by the police

who picked us up for questioning in Burdur as soon as it was known that we were asking for a one-time chauffeur whose original finds had led Mellaart to the site in the first place.

The chauffeur, the police claimed, had become a millionaire on the illegal sale of Hacilar artifacts. Why, then, had they never arrested him? They followed him all the time, they said, but they had never been able to catch him with the goods. And why, we asked, did they bother with us when they could go to Hacilar and collect the original thieves? Alas, said the chief commissioner, they are not in our district. We never caught up with the chauffeur. His brother, who was taking us to meet him, vanished as soon as the police appeared. The chauffeur is in fact a middleman who sells to dealers and private collectors.

There seems to be a curious anomaly in Turkish law that permits recognized collectors to obtain treasures that must, in the first place, have been illegally acquired. If you are caught stealing on a site, it means a short term of imprisonment or a small fine. But

if the glass cases in your house display a wide collection of antiquities that could only have been found in Turkish soil, you are somehow immune from any punishment.

The next stage in the smuggling trail was found in Izmir. There, we were taken to an antique dealer's shop in the jewelry district of Başmane. It was run by three brothers, and the ground floor appeared to be filled with innocuous bric-a-brac. At the top of a narrow staircase at the back, however, there was a small room which was entered by invitation only.

In that room we sat at a desk which, within five minutes, was covered with more than thirty thousand dollars worth of antiquities. To judge by the secrecy involved with their appearance, few of them had been legally purchased. On the desk were set out a standing Hacilar goddess ($3,300), a squatting Hacilar goddess ($1,700), an Assyrian seal ($1,000), two Yortan vases, a Roman Cybele, a silver nose-shield and gold dress ornaments from Greece, a silver "duck's head" vase and a gold laurel wreath from Lydia,

plus a few other trinkets.

The brothers told us that their main customer was an American dealer who has an antiquities business on the Continent and is a scholar in certain fields of archaeology. Any other top customers? "Yes, Hugo Weissmann." Weissmann is an international dealer, with a London home, who sold the British Museum its first two Hacilar pots. (Sir Frank Francis, Director of the British Museum, acknowledges this. "But what are we to do?" he asks. "If we don't take up offers like that, they only go to the Louvre or the Metropolitan in New York, and then we get into trouble for being dull and unenterprising.")

Weissmann, a small, gray-haired man in his sixties, says he is retired but is still in the market for the odd bargain. He denies the Izmir connection. "I haven't been there for six years. The Turks like to drop names to impress other customers. It's true I did sell the British Museum and the Ashmolean their Hacilar goddesses, but they came from a collection on an

Austrian estate near the Hungarian border. Their owner is an old friend.

"Most of those objects came out of Turkey in 1938, long before export restrictions were imposed. At that time Hacilar painted pottery was appearing in Europe. No one had any idea of its value. You used to be able to take it to a Turkish post office in an open parcel—they were looking for gold— and when they saw it was just a pot, that was okay."

Although Weissmann is not involved, at least he is aware of the methods the smugglers employ. "The crooked dealers never carry money and never carry the goods. They appear in Izmir, make contact with the local sellers, and are then usually taken to a house in the suburbs. The local men never keep the material in their shops.

"The visitor picks out the stuff he wants and settles on a price—he'll pay the price into an account in Switzerland later. He then goes to Istanbul and looks for the transporter. This is a man who can get anything out of Turkey. Not just through the post office. He must use other means. I know he's been able to export Hellenistic bronze statues four feet high."

Weissmann's wife pleaded with him not to name the transporter to us. "If you do," she said, "you know what could happen to you." Mr. Weissmann did know: he recalled the stories of three informers who had finished up stabbed to death in the back alleys of Aleppo, Homs, and Beirut.

Less ambitious collectors of Turkish antiquities can avoid getting involved with the transporter. A visit to the Covered Bazaar in Istanbul could be profitable. When we mentioned the word neolithic to a firm of dealers there, and they realized we were after something a little more special than their usual line, they pulled down the blind, locked the door, and produced from a safe a goddess which was going for $300.

"We have to be very careful," said the young English-speaking assistant.

"We are not supposed to have these things. They should be in the museums." But if we bought, we said, how would we get it out of the country? "Oh, that's easy," he answered. "It goes out through the American Army Post Office in Izmir. Their things don't have to go through the Customs."

But the U.S. Army Post Office is not the only staging point for the disappearing antiquities. Seven miles north of Izmir lies the airport of Çiğli, described by the Turkish government as "a field with American installations" and by the Turkish opposition as "an American base." It is in continual use as a terminus for jet charter flights, and Turkish Customs examination is never too strict where the giant inflow of tourist dollars is concerned. Çiğli is also used by the dealers.

We have focused attention on the smugglers' route from Hacilar because of its association with Mellaart, but there is much bigger game in the field. The Turks might well ask, for example, how half the valuable Kumlica Byzantine silver hoard, all of which was discovered hidden in a well near Antalya, comes to be in the possession of the Dumbarton Oaks Collection in Washington, D.C.

The Dorak mystery, which is really only one episode in the drama of smuggled antiquities, remains unsolved. Three possible solutions exist:

1) Mellaart *was* involved with Anna Papastrati in digging up the treasure and in its subsequent disappearance.

2) The whole thing was a hoax. Mellaart invented all the incidents, fabricated the sketches, and wrote up his "discovery" in an effort to raise his prestige in the eyes of his colleagues.

3) The girl was a plant, given a deliberate setup in Turkey to lead Mellaart to a faked collection in Izmir and eventually to discredit him.

The police evidence in the dossier at Mustafakemalpasha appears to us to dispose of the first theory. The second explanation is also most unlikely. It presupposes that Mellaart was in need of prestige at that point. In fact, in 1958, he was well on the way to fame.

The third suggestion appears to us to bear a hint of the truth. We have had discussions in London with dealers, leading museum authorities, and other experts, and they have suggested that it was the work of a gang of dealers, foreign and Turkish, prepared to pull off a gigantic smuggling operation. The idea is that they assembled in Izmir a collection of artifacts most of which were genuine and found near Dorak, but some of which could have been the contents of other graves. With the "treasure" amassed, the next requirement was an acknowledgement of its existence by some authority whose word would be unchallenged. Anyone in the antiquities business would know that Mellaart was their man.

It would then be a simple step to plot his movements, plant the girl on the train, and lead Mellaart to "217 Kazim Direk Street" in Izmir. Mellaart's obsessive drive would do the rest. The gang would then be free to remove the Dorak hoard from Turkey, wait until Mellaart's article was published in London and the news of the treasure spread throughout the world, and sell out at once to the first unsuspecting millionaire.

What then, as far as Turkey is concerned, is the answer to operations like this, and the hundred smaller exercises that occur each year? Burhan Tezcan, the Director of Excavations in the Department of Antiquities, was once reported to have said in frustration: "All foreign archaeologists should be banned from Turkey." This would hardly stop the smuggling trade, but the threat gives foreign archaeologists and their sponsoring museums and societies a vital stake in finding some solution.

Turkey's present laws governing the movement of antiquities are no help. The almost complete prohibition of the export of artifacts merely exag-

gerates the shortage of supply; a shortage which the international gangs meet with smuggling and forgery. Ankara should learn from Egypt. There, mixed committees examine the results of annual excavations to decide which objects should remain at home and which may be exported. In this way the Egyptians ensure a steady stream of antiquities to museums abroad and the foreign archaeologist feels recompensed for his labor.

There is another, more immediate solution: tighter security. When the Turkish authorities are asked why they do not guard *all* their archaeological sites, they point out the expense of doing so. But this is an economic fallacy: the value of what the country is losing each year would pay for a comprehensive security system ten times over.

Meanwhile the rape of Turkey goes on. Italian and American yachts, evading Turkish coast guard patrols, have been known to slip inshore, close to the ruins of the Roman town of Side under cover of night, and with their crews, dynamite Greek and Roman antiquities from their setting.

The loss dismays the Turks. An official in Istanbul's Archaeological Museum said: "I have given up hope for Turkey. You *must* write your article. Perhaps UNESCO will see it and some international agreement will be arranged. If not, everything will be gone. In ten years' time in Turkey, there will be nothing."

Kenneth Pearson and Patricia Connor, both writers for the London Sunday Times, *traveled hundreds of miles in Turkey interviewing the principal characters in the Dorak affair. Mr. Pearson was a member of an award-winning team of newsmen in 1966. Miss Connor, a graduate of Bristol University, has also written for the BBC.*

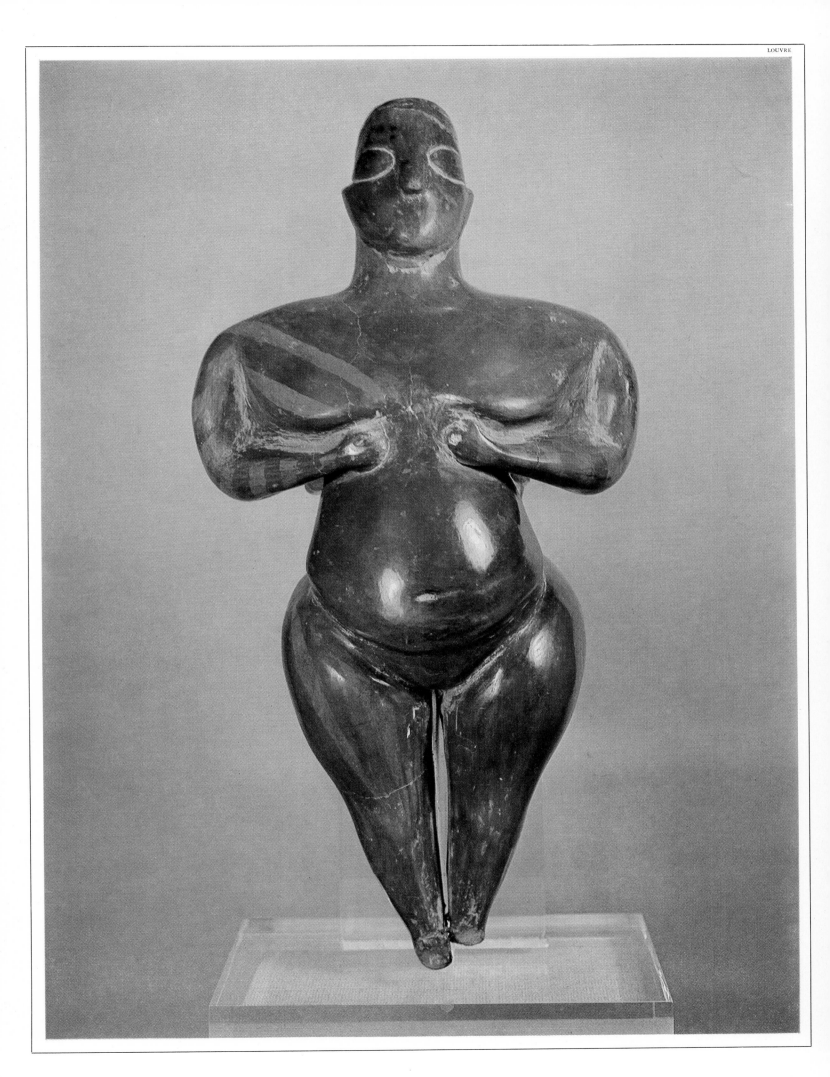

THE LITERARY ROAD TO

ROME

The city has always attracted writers.
They have mourned its fall
and complained about its decadence—
and have never stopped coming

By Norman Kotker

Photographed for Horizon by Sonja Bullaty and Angelo Lomeo

Rome, as any Roman can tell you, is the most interesting city in the world. What other place controls the keys to the kingdom of heaven, and kept for so long those to the kingdom of earth as well. Over the centuries the ancient capital of the world has exerted a powerful attraction on tourists—particularly on writers, who have come to seek inspiration among its ruins. Traveling from distant towns—London, Paris, Frankfurt —that had once been under Roman sway, they came to view the dead city, to mourn the fall of its great empire and to grieve over the decadence of its church. Mourning has always seemed the appropriate attitude for writers to adopt in Rome. "Rome its own sad sepulchre appears," declaimed Washington Irving as he entered the city for the first time. ". . . death seems to have been born in Rome," Chateaubriand mused as he walked along the Appian Way.

But most writers found to their surprise that they came to expend more sorrow over Rome's life than they did over its death. They loved the ruins, but almost everything else tended to shock them. They found the Romans decadent, the shop-keepers avaricious, the aristocrats snobbish, the children diseased, and the fleas healthy. As travelers will, they lost their purses, their tempers, their appetites, and even in the cases of Tasso and Keats, their lives. But they rarely lost their point of view. A few, of course, had happier reactions. Petrarch held the city in reverence, and Stendhal was amused by it; Goethe was delighted by the robust sensuality of the Romans. Tolerant or not, all of the writers described their experiences. Their opinions of Rome, and photographs of places associated with their visits—places that often have changed remarkably little since their times—appear on the following pages.

The literary road to Rome has invariably led to the city's ruins and churches. Here, the Palatine Hill, with the dome of St. Peter's visible at upper left.

THE ELUSIVE LAUREL

On Easter Sunday, 1341, the poet Petrarch ascended the Capitoline Hill above the ruins of the Forum to be crowned poet laureate, the first poet to receive the honor from the Roman people since antiquity. He had traveled

Dante and a laurel-crowned Petrarch

from his home in Provence for the occasion. Preceded by twelve aristocratic youths dressed in red, six nobles bearing crowns of flowers, and a Senator carrying a wreath of laurel, Petrarch entered the assembly hall of the city to the sound of trumpets and fifes. "Long live the Senators!" he shouted three times, and then recited a sonnet in honor of the ancient Romans. His audience responded with delight, crying "Long live the Capitol and the poet!" Soon after, Petrarch deposited his laurel wreath in the Vatican and went home to write a series of penitential poems and a book in which he castigated himself for his faults, not the least of which was his great craving for acclaim.

Dante shared Petrarch's craving, although he wanted to be crowned poet laureate in his native city of Florence rather than in Rome. He never got his wish. But he apparently visited Rome at least once, a few years earlier than Petrarch, and prided himself on being of "the holy seed of the Romans." He believed that the feuds that rent Florence (and that sent him into exile for life) were fought between the descendants of the Roman troops who settled in Florence in the first century B.C. and the offspring of the Etruscan natives of the city. The poet had a typically exalted idea of the glory of Rome; to him the city symbolized the Church's rule over the world. But it was in his time that the popes abandoned their traditional residence, the Lateran Palace, to move to Avignon in southern France. Dante considered this defection a sin, punishable by eternal damnation. In the *Divine Comedy* he assigned a special place in hell for a pope who left the city for Avignon, Clement V, whom he called "that great cheat." Several other popes got no better treatment; they suffered in hell hanging upside down in a travesty of baptism, being purified with fire instead of holy water. For although Dante, like many later writers, considered Rome inspiring in theory, he had little but contempt for the decadent realities of the city's life. He thought it appropriate to compare the sinners being run through a gantlet of devils in hell as punishment for fraud, to the supposedly devout pilgrims who crowded across the Sant' Angelo bridge over the Tiber to visit the shrine of Saint Peter at the Vatican.

A bookstand in the Tasso museum at Sant' Onofrio.

Two centuries later the poet Torquato Tasso came to Rome from the court of Ferrara to be crowned as Petrarch had been. Tasso had been insane on and off for the previous twenty years; he was afraid that his enemies were trying to poison him, an idea which, in Renaissance Italy, was not necessarily a manifestation of paranoia. Having been educated by the Jesuits, he was obsessed by the fear of heresy, and once denounced himself to the Inquisition as a possible heretic. The Inquisition let him go; and when a new pope, Clement VIII, offered in 1594 to crown him with laurel for his epic poetry, Tasso saw it as an assurance that his faith was pure, and that he would be rewarded with a halo in heaven as well. As it turned out Tasso received his heavenly reward before he could enjoy his earthly one. When the time came for him to be crowned, he was too sick to attend the ceremony; he lay dying at the monastery of Sant' Onofrio, high on one of the seven hills of Rome, where he had sought refuge in order to be as close to heaven as possible.

The Sant' Angelo bridge, over which pilgrims went to St. Peter's

To Dante's distress the popes abandoned their residence at the Lateran Palace. Opposite, the Lateran Cloisters—still deserted.

THE HISTORIANS' ROME

"My temper is not very susceptible of enthusiasm..." wrote the English historian Edward Gibbon as he recalled his visit to Rome in 1764. "But at the distance of twenty-five years I can neither forget nor express the strong emotions which agitated my mind as I first approached and entered the *Eternal City*. After a sleepless night I trod, with a lofty step, the ruins of the Forum . . . and several days of intoxication were lost or enjoyed before I could descend to a cool and minute investigation." Gibbon devoted his

cool and minute attention—which was to result in his *Decline and Fall of the Roman Empire*—to the church of modern Rome as well as to the ruins of the ancient city; and he came to the conclusion that it was the church and the decadent religion of Christianity boring from within, rather than the barbarians attacking from without, that had caused the fall of Rome.

A famous passage in his autobiography describes the moment in the church of Ara Coeli (below) on the Capitol when Gibbon first

decided to write his great history. "It was at Rome on the 15th of October 1764, as I sat musing amid the ruins of the Capitol, while the barefooted friars were singing vespers in the temple of Jupiter, that the idea of writing the decline and fall of the city first started to my mind." Later and lesser historians, delving in the ruins of Rome, have gleefully pointed out that Gibbon was wrong; it was the temple of Juno that stood on the site. But they have hardly had the same success in demolishing his theories.

A century after Gibbon's visit another young and impressionable historian, Henry Adams, came to the city; in recollection of his noted predecessor, he spent hours sitting on the steps of the church of Ara Coeli thinking about history. Though Adams disagreed with Gibbon's theories, he could find no better ones. "Rome could not be

Gibbon in 1764

fitted into an orderly, middle-class, Bostonian, systematic scheme of evolution. No law of progress applied to it. Not even time sequences—that last refuge of helpless historians—had value for it." Rome did not evolve, the historian concluded; it just existed. Its history was a series of experiments that had failed, much as England, the great empire of Adams's time, was beginning to fail; and as America, the next great empire, would probably fail too.

But, like Gibbon, most historians have found meaning in Roman history, and when they haven't seen a meaning, they have read one into it. They have usually linked the fate of the city with the will of heaven, or at least, as Gibbon did, with the representatives of heaven on earth. One of the first was the ancient Roman historian Livy,

It was during a service in the church of Ara Coeli that Gibbon resolved to write The Decline and Fall of the Roman Empire.

Machiavelli

who pointed out with pride that his city ruled the mightiest of empires next to that of heaven and implied that it was, naturally, heaven's will that made this possible.

Heaven was called on to witness just the opposite point of view by Saint Augustine, who lived in the early fifth century, the time when the city of Rome was overrun by the Visigoths. Augustine spent a year in Rome as a young man; its fall was inevitable, he said, for Rome was the city of man—it was mortal and it would die. Only the city of

God was eternal. Like most historical generalizations, this remains unproved. Later ages, disagreeing with Augustine, would call Rome the "Eternal City"; and its survival was due primarily to the efforts of Augustine's church.

A less stoical witness to Rome's decay was Niccolò Machiavelli—a minor and ineffective diplomat representing an impotent principality at a time when Italy was at the mercy of the other nations of Europe. Like Dante, he was a Florentine, and he considered himself a descendant of the ancient Romans. He was horrified by the difference between ancient and modern Italy; and he longed to restore Rome to power, with a Roman dictator ruling the country, a Roman-style army protecting it from the Gauls (who, led by Charles VIII of France, had just sent

Rome's independent nobles stood in the way of Machiavelli's dream of a unified Italy. Above, the palace-fortress of one noble clan, the Savelli, built on the ruins of a Roman theatre.

an invading army over the Alps), and re-Romanized citizens, who would once again demonstrate the sturdy virtues that had made their ancestors rulers of the world.

Machiavelli scorned the papacy, believing it to be the cause of Italy's break-up into a group of feuding principalities; but he was practical enough to see it as the strongest force in the peninsula and longed to enlist it for more mundane purposes than those to which it was ostensibly dedicated. It was from the Church that he hoped to draw the man who would be Italy's savior. His model was Caesar Borgia, Pope Alexander VI's bastard son, who had driven the noble Roman families out of their fortresses built among the city's ruins, and who was beginning to carve out an empire for himself like that other Roman Caesar, Julius. The modern Caesar fell, however, before he was able to consolidate his power, leaving Machiavelli disappointed but not without hope. He refused

to surrender his fantasy and incorporated it into a guidebook for rulers, *The Prince;* the treatise was dedicated to a Florentine relative of Pope Leo X, whom Machiavelli hoped would pick up

Henry Adams

where Caesar Borgia left off. He didn't. It was not until centuries after Machiavelli's death that another Caesar, Mussolini, attempted to bring the historian's fantasy to life. He learned to his sorrow what Machiavelli could never accept: the glory of Rome had vanished.

On the steps of the church of Ara Coeli Henry Adams mused about the history of Rome—and the future of America.

When Goethe came to Rome for the first time in October, 1786, he realized a lifelong dream. Throughout his youth he had heard his father describe the glories of Italy, attention with descriptions of Italian art, so superior to its German counterpart, and of Italian women, who might be no more liberal in offering their favors than German sentimental novel of love, and of *Götz*, a wildly popular play that glorified the German virtues of force and national pride. He had also made a reputation as a Geheimrat—roughly equivalent to a prime minister—of the minor duchy of Weimar. He had been appointed to the post by a princeling afire with the ideals of the Enlightenment—roughly the same impulses that had inspired greater sovereigns, Catherine the Great of Russia and Frederick the Great of Prussia, to consult Voltaire on how to rule. But fame and high position had failed to make Goethe happy. Indeed, in his old age he complained that he had been happy for only four weeks in his entire life, and he lived to be eighty-three. Those weeks were probably spent in Rome.

Goethe left Weimar one day, supposedly for a brief visit to a spa in Bohemia. When his employer, the Duke, next heard from him, he was in Italy requesting a leave of absence in order to study art. His request was granted. Goethe took up residence in Rome under a pseudonym, Filippo Möller, and pretended to be a painter. But his disguise fooled no one. To the authorities he was still Geheimrat Goethe, and they watched him closely, presuming with baroque logic that no prime minister would ever pose as a painter just for the sake of painting; there had to be a more artful reason. The papal police, in the pay of the Austrian emperor, searched his rooms and read his correspondence, looking for information about political intrigues in Weimar. They discovered nothing that was incriminating, for with his journey to Rome, Goethe had abandoned his interest in the government of Weimar. He had always wanted to be an artist; in Rome he lived the Bohemian artist's life as best he could, affecting the wide-brimmed "Rembrandt" hat (see portrait at left) that the painters of the time loved

Goethe liked to contemplate the ruins of antiquity such as those of the imperial aqueduct (below).

for the elder Goethe's visit had been the high spot of his rather uneventful life. He had little to say that could be of interest to his brilliant and enigmatic son; but he could catch the young man's girls, but who were far more liberated when they did. By the time Goethe arrived in Italy, at the age of thirty-seven, he was already famous as the author of *The Sorrows of Young Werther*, a

Goethe at his Roman window

The Egyptian obelisk

to wear. He spent his days with other artists and visited the picture galleries. He drew —everything from standard views of St. Peter's to sketches of the hieroglyphs on an Egyptian obelisk that had just been unearthed. (He made a special point of copying the hieroglyphs on top of the obelisk, which had been visible before only to the sun-god.) He frequented the artists' taverns and talked endlessly about painting; and, as a proper Bohemian should, he made love.

His mistress was a young Roman girl whom he supported—an arrangement that was characteristic of all levels of society in eighteenth-century Rome. "Everything in Rome has a price," the ancient satirist Juvenal had written, and for century after century, in letter after letter, writers had echoed him, complaining about the city's decadence. Crotchety as he was about almost everything else, Goethe did not agree. He was delighted to live "among a sensual people." His book *The Sorrows of Young Werther* had been about love, but that was a chaste, romantic, northern love that had ended with suicide. This kind of love was quite different. "Still do I mark the churches, palaces, ruins, and columns,/ As a wise traveler should . . ." Goethe wrote later in one of his Roman Elegies. "Soon all this will be past; and then will there be but *one* temple,/ Amor's temple alone . . ."

The poet gave his mistress a classical name, because he saw in her limbs the beauty of classical antiquity. The name was Faustina. It was an odd choice; Goethe had already written, although he had not yet published, the first version of *Faust*. The girl sold herself to Goethe as Faust sold himself to the devil; and it is with Mephistopheles that Goethe more and more identified himself while he was writing the book. But it is impossible to learn the exact connection. It is enough to know that Goethe, unlike so many other writers, did not feel cheated by Rome. His liaison with Faustina lasted for much of the year that he spent in the city.

But eventually he left the "sensual" Romans to return to Germany. Back in Weimar, he refused to resume his career as a government official. Mining reports and committee meetings to discuss the state of the public highways were abandoned for good. His contemporaries found this puzzling; but to the modern mind it is easy to understand why a writer—after having seen Rome fallen into decay—would refuse to pose as a prime minister.

DEATH OF A POET

Rome's most notable literary visitor came to the city not for inspiration but to save his life. John Keats arrived in Italy in 1819, on his twenty-fifth birthday, dying from the consumption that had already carried off his mother

But Keats ignored their invitation; he had never really liked Shelley nor enjoyed his company. He resolved to go to Italy, but remained vague about plans to visit Pisa.

Accompanied by a friend, the painter Joseph Severn, he

again. He decided to commit suicide; he had seen consumptives die before. But Severn caught him with a bottle of poison in his hand and snatched it away. For weeks, as his friend grew weaker, Severn watched by the bedside, tending the patient carefully and writing frantically to England to ask for money. To pass the time, Severn sometimes sketched. "28th Jan. 3 o'clock Mg.," he wrote beneath a drawing (below, left) of the dying poet. "Drawn to keep me awake—a deadly sweat

gated and the furniture burned, as the Roman quarantine laws demanded. The body was buried in the Protestant cemetery, under a gravestone showing a Grecian lyre with half its strings broken, a device that had been designed for it by Severn at Keats's request.

When Shelley heard of the death, he was outraged. He attributed it—romantic that he was—to the cruelty of the English reviewers who had mocked Keats's work. In "Adonais," Shelley's elegy for Keats, he harangued critics

From his sickroom Keats saw the Spanish Steps

and a brother. Keats was a doctor—although he had abandoned that career for poetry—and he was able to diagnose his case and predict its course from the first moment he coughed up blood. He had just published the odes that would make him immortal; but they had not

went almost directly to Rome and took rooms with a view of the Spanish Steps (shown above). His first weeks were pleasant enough. In the warm Roman sunshine Keats seemed to be doing better. His rooms were comfortable, and he met an agreeable group of English visitors with whom he socialized. But the irritability and nervousness that accompany the final stages of tuberculosis soon began to prey on Keats's spirits. He had always been a sociable person, but he now refused to go out any more for strolls in the Pincio Gardens. He blamed Napoleon's sister Pauline, the Princess Borghese, for this; he was annoyed, and doubtless jealous, because she was flirting with one of his companions, a tall and handsome English lieutenant. He himself was short and had always been sensitive about it.

Early in December, 1819, Keats had an attack of coughing and began to spit blood

Severn portrayed Shelley writing among the ruins of the Baths of Caracalla.

was on him all this night."

Early in his life Keats had abandoned faith in Christianity. But now that he was dying, he grew frightened and depressed at his lack of faith, that "last cheap comfort, which every rogue and fool may have." Even the noble example of Socrates, one of his idols, failed to console him. Patiently he described to Severn the consumptive's final agony so that he would not be shocked by what he was about to witness. On February 23 he died. The house was fumi-

who had questioned Keats's talent. "Go thou to Rome," he admonished— the doubters would see immediately that the poet's grave conferred distinction on the city. The same could be said of Shelley himself after he drowned a year later—carrying a book of Keats's poetry, which was burned with him on his funeral pyre. Supposedly only his heart was saved, snatched from the fire by Lord Byron. That was carried to Rome and buried near the body of Keats and the grave of Shelley's child.

Keats on his deathbed

been well received, and in the last months of his life his greatest pain came from the fear that he would not live "among the English poets." He had been invited to Italy by Shelley and his wife, who were staying at Pisa. They had recently left Rome, where they had seen their three-year-old son fall sick and die.

"A thing of beauty is a joy forever." The first line of "Endymion" is barely visible at upper left in a framed manuscript of the poem that hangs in the Keats Memorial in Rome. Buildings of the Piazza di Spagna and a fresh rose are reflected in the glass.

"We have just returned from St. Peter's," wrote Stendhal in his *Roman Journal* in an entry dated Christmas Day, 1827. "The ceremony was magnificent. There were perhaps a hundred English ladies, several of them of the rarest beauty.... His Holiness designated a cardinal to say mass in his stead. The Saviour's blood was brought to

Stendhal

the pope seated on his throne behind the altar, and he sucked it with a gold straw. I have never seen anything so imposing."

The city Stendhal was describing had been created by the Roman Church. The ancient ruins were there, of course; but they merely provided a picturesque backdrop for the hypocritical and wonderfully polished society of papal Rome. "The ices are excellent," he reports of an evening party at one of the great Roman *palazzi*, "the walls adorned with eight or ten paintings by great masters. The *brio* of the conversation disposes one to enjoy their merit. In order to be polite toward the sovereign one utters, on occasion, a few words in favor of God."

Stendhal himself was less than polite to the sovereign. "The pope's government is a

pure despotism," he wrote; it held out to its subjects "the gallows in this world and hell in the next." "The moment a father sees a child of his manifesting a spark of intelligence, he makes a priest of him.... Who knows? he may become pope." "The profound immorality that reigned in the Sacred College in 1800 has gradually disappeared, and so has all wit. In Rome as elsewhere, it is the most stupid who govern..."

Stendhal's *Roman Journal* is as stylish and gossipy as the city it describes, and as hypocritical: it is neither Roman nor a journal. It was written in Paris, more than fifteen years after Stendhal had last seen Rome. In desperate need of money, he worked it up from hazy memories, from library research, and from the notes of a cousin who had just returned from Italy. The book could, with some justice, be called Stendhal's first great work of fiction. Episodes are invented, and cardinals and countesses created, to suit the author's fancy. Works of art are described in detail from dim memories or from engravings and the descriptions of other travelers. Stendhal's sources may not have been original, but his judgments on art certainly were. One Poussin picture he finds "an estimable painting but highly disagreeable to look at." "Almost all the statues placed in St. Peter's are ridiculous," he proclaims. One of them, Michelangelo's *Pietà*, inspired him with some new thoughts on a son's obligations to his mother. "If Jesus had the slightest feeling of gratitude" for Mary, Stendhal says, he ought to have spared her the sight of his wounds.

Stendhal had had a very good chance to view Roman

This room in the Quirinal Palace still contains a cast of the frieze ordered by Napoleon.

art when he first visited the city in 1811; for he stayed at the Quirinal palace (above), once a papal residence and now the official home of the president of Italy. He was there as a guest of his cousin, Martial Daru, whom Napoleon had sent to Rome with the title of "Intendant of Crown Properties." To Napoleon, crown property was everything he could lay his hands on; and Daru was charged with the task of sending classical art—the *Apollo Belvedere*, the *Lao-*

coön, the *Medici Venus*—back to Paris for the new imperial museum at the Louvre. Stendhal was not one to be shocked by this looting. He had been doing the same thing as an officer in the French army in Germany. Besides, he idolized Napoleon. When he visited Rome, the Quirinal was "the Emperor's Palace"; there, in honor of his conquests, Napoleon had commissioned a plaster frieze in one of the state rooms, depicting the triumphs of his own idol,

A ceremonial welcome greeted Chateaubriand (on left of woman at center) when he came to Rome in 1827 as French ambassador

Alexander the Great. By the time Stendhal wrote his Roman journal, the palace was once again the pope's. The frieze remained, but the imperial splendor had gone. The pope or his servants, Stendhal reports, were so un-imperial that they were accustomed to hanging the papal laundry out of the palace window to dry.

During the year and a half in which Stendhal was ostensibly in Rome writing his travel journal, another French writer, the historian Chateaubriand, actually *was* there, serving as his country's ambassador to the pope. Chateaubriand did not share Stendhal's view of the city. His was the romantic's Rome —a dead city where he could wallow in "profound melancholy" as much as he liked. "There are more tombs than dead in this city," he wrote, and he hoped some day to fill one of them. He made plans to spend his old age writing his memoirs in the monastery of Sant' Onofrio. Like most of his romantic fantasies, this never came to pass.

Chateaubriand had his first taste of death in Rome years earlier, in 1803, while he was serving Napoleon as the First Secretary of the French embassy. He had been accompanied by his mistress, the Countess de Beaumont, a pale and consumptive aristocrat, the first in that "funeral procession of ... women" whom the writer had loved. The couple had difficulty in finding a house: "... there is a prejudice in Rome against diseases of the chest, which are held to be infectious." Like Keats, Mme de Beaumont improved at first in the mild Roman climate. But the improvement did not last. "One day I took her to the Colosseum," Chateaubriand wrote later in his *Memoirs*. "She managed to get out of the carriage, and went and sat on a stone facing one of the altars placed in the precincts of the building. She raised her eyes and looked slowly round those porticoes which had themselves been dead so many years, and which had seen so many die ... The dying woman then lowered her eyes step by step, from the sun down to the arena, fixed them on the altar cross, and said to me: 'Let us go: I am cold.' I took her home; she went to bed and never rose again." The funeral was splendid, arranged with a pomp that was characteristic of Rome. Chateaubriand noted with pride that Napoleon's sister, the Princess Borghese, lent her family hearse.

Chateaubriand's mistress died after seeing the cross at the center of the Colosseum that commemorated the early Christian martyrs.

27

"A PECULIAR QUALITY OF MALIGNITY"

"...I have seldom or never spent so wretched a time anywhere," wrote Nathaniel Hawthorne during his first days in Rome. "The atmosphere certainly has a peculiar quality of malignity." The streets were "indescribably ugly," and he was repelled by the "...sour bread ...enormous prices for poor living; beggars, pickpockets, ancient temples and broken monuments...a shabby pop-

Nathaniel Hawthorne

ulation, smoking bad cigars." Hawthorne considered Rome dirty, as many Americans do, and he wondered "whether the ancient Romans were as unclean a people as we everywhere find those who have succeeded them."

Hawthorne arrived in the city in February of 1858, having come to Italy for the sake of the health of his wife and daughter. He was immediately attacked not only by flu but by the fleas for which the city was famous. Even though he huddled by the fire in his room with all his coats on, he was unable to get warm. There were no "great logs of a New England forest to burn" in Rome, he observed sadly. Occasionally he went to St. Peter's, which was the only place he could find that was not too cold. But he rarely went out. However, as the climate changed, he became happier.

"I am very glad I have seen the pope," he wrote at the end of March, "because now he may be crossed out of the list of sights to be seen." The list of sights was enormous, and, according to the custom of the time, Hawthorne and his wife added to it the studios of painters and sculptors working there. They sought out Browning's friend William Wetmore Story, whose apartments in the Palazzo Barberini were a center for American artists and writers in Rome. Among those who visited Story were Ralph Waldo Emerson and that original Boston bluestocking, Margaret Fuller; the lady abolitionists Julia Ward Howe and Harriet Beecher Stowe; and Henry Wadsworth Longfellow (who posed for his portrait by G. P. A. Healy, at right, beneath the Arch of Titus). Hawthorne crossed paths with none of these literary compatriots, but he did encounter the poet William Cullen Bryant. The two men spent an evening together, discussing Bleeding Kansas.

Although Hawthorne was too preoccupied to work while he was in Rome, because of the mortal illness of his daughter Una, he did think of ideas for two stories. One was inspired by a macabre newspaper report about a widower who had had his late wife's ashes chemically resolved into a stone, which he had set in a ring; Hawthorne's sentimental protagonist would present the ring as a bridal gift to his next spouse. The second story became *The Marble Faun*. Its theme is certainly less ghoulish, yet the novel does evoke the "peculiar quality of malignity" the author found in Rome. A climactic scene is set in the Cemetery

of the Capuchins (opposite), one of Rome's more sensational tourist sights, where the walls are adorned with the skulls of monks who have departed to dwell in the City of God. Since the hero of *The Marble Faun* had killed a sinister Capuchin who was plaguing the heroine, the exigencies of nineteenth-century fiction required that he and his lady visit the cemetery where the remains of the victim would soon lie.

Most of *The Marble Faun* is set in Rome, and the book was written shortly after Hawthorne left the city. It is surprising that he survived to write it at all; when he departed, he records, the servants who had waited on his family "cursed us plentifully, —wishing that we might never come to our journey's

The heroine of The Marble Faun

end, and that we might all break our necks or die of apoplexy,—the most awful curse that an Italian knows ...it precludes the possibility of extreme unction."

Longfellow and his daughter Edith under the Arch of Titus

The skulls of monks adorn the walls of vaults beneath the Capuchin church, one of Hawthorne's favorite Roman haunts.

LOVE AMONG THE RUINS

"So Robert Browning and Elizabeth Barrett have gone off together!" wrote Wordsworth in 1846 when he was told that the two poets had eloped to Italy. "It is to be hoped they can understand each other, for no one else

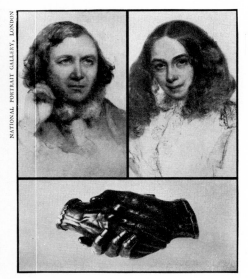

The Brownings—and a bronze cast of their clasped hands taken in Rome, 1853.

can." Apparently they did, for their life was happy, and they found themselves admired and welcomed wherever they traveled.

They went first to Pisa and then to Florence, where they lived for a time in rooms adorned with a portrait of Dante and a cast of Keats's death mask. They had come to Italy hoping to restore Elizabeth's faltering health; soon, instead of being confined to a parlor sofa, she was able to go mountain climbing.

They spent the next ten years in Italy, mostly in Florence. But there were occasional stays in Rome, where the Brownings enjoyed the company of such luminaries as Thackeray, Hans Christian Andersen, and their friend William Wetmore Story. The city itself figures in several of Browning's poems,

the most famous of which is "The Bishop Orders his Tomb in St. Praxed's." Naturally enough, the poem is about death.

The life of the two lovers was idyllic, except for their continued worries about Elizabeth's health and that of their young son, whose nickname was, aptly enough, "Pen"—"a poetical child," his mother called him in a letter to a friend from Rome. In the letter she proclaimed her thankfulness that, despite her fears, the little boy "had not dropped a single rose-leaf from his cheeks." Eventually, back in Rome during the last winter of her life, she was dropping her own rose leaves. During that winter Elizabeth was grieving over the recent death of her sister in London. (One of the few things that cheered her was a letter of condolence from Harriet Beecher Stowe.) While Browning went for long walks beside the Tiber, she would rest indoors, waiting impatiently for him to come home, and when he did, would nag him gently for not spending more

time at home writing. Tennyson spent a certain part of each day rigidly devoted to nothing but work, she reminded him; why couldn't Browning? By the end of the winter, Browning was forced to co-operate, for Elizabeth had entered the final stages of her illness. Unlike Keats, she had enough strength to leave the city, and on June 4, 1861, the couple started out for Florence. By the end of the month she was dead.

Death, not love, was what Dickens saw when he came to Rome a year or so before the Brownings first arrived. It was typical of Dickens—whose fascination with prisons and crime was unending—that one of the first tourist attractions he attended was a public execution. He was horrified to note that the people in the audience counted the drops of blood that spurted out of the decapitated criminal's neck in order to bet that number in the public lottery. Roman superstition astonished him. He carefully noted the menu (fish, vegetables, and two kinds of wine) served at a

Charles Dickens, 1830

ceremony in which the pope and twelve men dressed as apostles re-enacted the Last Supper. And he wondered why pilgrims in the Colosseum always paid their devotions to one cross, which provided them with an indulgence for their sins for a hundred days when they kissed it, even though nearby there was another cross—almost neglected—which offered the faithful two hundred and forty days of indulgence for a kiss.

No doubt the Romans, between sins, are still kissing the hundred-day cross. But modern writers don't seem to be interested. They are much too busy documenting the sins of Rome. As romantic writers went there to view death, their successors go to view life; i.e., sex, which obsesses this century as much as death obsessed the last. Love affairs, like that of the innocent Brownings are more at home in Paris today. If art is any valid measure, it is evident that sex, or what the Italians call an "*avventura*," is the thing for Rome. Tourists no longer have to go to Italy, or even read a book, to catch a view of love among the ruins. As the film replaces the written word, Rome in all its decadence can come to them. Now, thanks to the work of such latter-day Roman journalists as Federico Fellini and Michelangelo Antonioni, the city is apparently even more fallen than Gibbon's Rome, more wicked than Stendhal's, more malignant than Hawthorne's—all of which may explain why the parade of writers shows not the least sign of slackening.

Norman Kotker, formerly on the staff of HORIZON *is now the Editor of* HORIZON *books.*

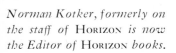

The Renaissance tomb of a bishop in St. Praxed's church resembles the one described in Browning's poem

The Whitney Museum at Night

BREUER: THE LAST "MODERN" ARCHITECT

The first impression of New York's new Whitney Museum of American Art, as it neared completion last summer, was discouraging. With its massive, raw cantilevers, the building loomed out over a sunken, moat-like sculpture garden; curious trapezoidal windows were punched in the façade; concrete blinder-walls went up at either side, cutting off the adjacent apartment houses.

Its appearance began to improve as a handsome veneer of gray granite was set in place over the concrete and the scaffolding was removed. Still, right up to opening night late last September, the sidewalk superintendents were having a field day, dubbing the museum everything from an upside-down ziggurat to a *Kunst* bunker. All signs pointed to another of those architectural controversies such as the one that greeted Frank Lloyd Wright's spiral Guggenheim Museum a few years earlier.

For most New York critics and artists, the inauguration festivities were their introduction to the work of Marcel Breuer, the Hungarian-born and Bauhaus-trained architect who has been practicing in the United States since the late 1930's. The building, on firsthand inspection, turned out to be a delightful surprise. "I even like the

floors," one New York art critic said, shuffling his feet on the split bluestone. "They have the feel of probity."

What the opening night guests had discovered was that while the building seemed aggressive on the outside, the architectural style of the interior had been carefully planned to accommodate the basic function of the museum—the creation of an ideal display place for art. Spaces are well lighted and inviting. The ceiling is an open grid that allows the movable partitions to be arranged in a variety of ways at the same time that it incorporates air conditioning and elaborate lighting. Open loft spaces can, of course, seem like vast, echoing boxes, and Breuer had obviously set out to counteract this. His main weapon against monotony was as old as architecture itself: an orchestration of contrasting materials, surfaces, and finishes. Concrete is left exposed and textured by the imprint of the wooden forms or bushhammered to bring out the coarse gravel aggregate; bronze fittings are matched with teakwood railings; massive blocks of polished granite are used as benches or counters. All are typical Breuer touches. His use of surfaces gives the whole museum a hand-crafted feeling which, in an age when

By CRANSTON JONES

Breuer, in the Whitney

New York's Whitney Museum crowns a career that began forty years ago with a Bauhaus chair

architecture increasingly looks as if it could be turned out by the mile, is in itself a source of pleasure.

Such a vigorous aesthetic is not to everyone's immediate taste. *The New York Time*'s architectural critic, Ada Louise Huxtable, for instance, decided that a liking for it had to be acquired, "like olives and warm beer." "At first, second and third glance," she wrote, "the building suggests a mannered tour de force in the current mode of architecture for sculpture's sake. On fourth, fifth and further inspections, matching interior to exterior, it reveals itself as a carefully calculated design that squeezes the most out of a small awkward corner lot with maximum artistry and almost hypnotic skill."

Not only was the building, at least at the outset, puzzling to many, but the public also had great difficulty in placing Breuer. The reason, in part, is geography. Breuer has lived and practiced in Germany, Great Britain, and the United States; his major structures are scattered across this country, South America, and Europe. In part, too, he has been the victim of his own precocity. It is staggering to realize that Breuer, the man who designed the first tubular steel furniture more than forty years ago,

is today only sixty-five, an age when, in architecture, the greatest opportunities traditionally present themselves.

"Breuer is the last 'modern' architect," Philip Johnson, the architect and critic, commented recently. By this, of course, he meant that Breuer still continues to evolve from the principles and methodology that originated in the 1920's and are largely associated with the German Bauhaus. There, the ideal progression was from the design of a single piece of furniture to a room, a building, and finally to a town or city. It is a tribute to both his perseverance and his talents that such a progression happens to describe Breuer's professional career at a time when his work in progress ranges from a house for a Swiss art collector to a whole ski town, Flaine, in France's Haute-Savoie and includes as well the new Housing and Urban Development (HUD) headquarters in Washington; a Benedictine abbey and school in Minnesota and a new college in Bismarck, North Dakota; and a university laboratory for Yale.

Although the Bauhaus insisted that its goal was a rational approach to architecture, it in fact created such a powerful visual image of glass curtain-walls, immaculate

33

BREUER'S EARLY DESIGNS

The Bauhaus, designed by Walter Gropius when the school moved to Dessau in 1925, was in itself a declaration of the principles of modern architecture, incorporating gleaming glass curtain-walls and pristine white cubes. Breuer was commissioned to furnish the new quarters.

Breuer's most famous single furniture design—and the forerunner of countless outdoor pieces—was his 1928 chrome steel cantilever chair with bentwood frame and natural caning. Breuer saw it as functional and symbolic of technology itself.

The unit, or modular, kitchen embodied an idea revolutionary for its time—and gave Breuer his first commissions for interior design. Later he applied the same principle to big apartment-house projects.

white cubes, and gleaming chrome furniture that today the name brings to mind a style rather than an orderly method for solving design problems. But for Breuer the conflict between a style (by definition, a certain "look," frozen in set images) and an approach (which will produce increasingly varied solutions) is something that he brushes aside with impatience. He feels that "modern architecture" has less to do with white stucco finishes and boxes on stilts than with the flow of space within a building, the use of glass to establish interior-exterior continuities, the utilization of both the newest materials and the most traditional within a geometry that is distinctly man made (and not a romantic evocation), and the creation of buildings that are both expressive and functional.

Nothing, at first glance, could seem farther removed from Breuer's famous 1928 cantilever chair—the forerunner of an endless number of outdoor garden chairs—than the looming cantilevers of the Whitney Museum. When I spoke to him of the contrast, he explained the similarity of principle: "I have always been attracted to the idea of architecture as monumental sculpture. I have always been strict about function, and I still believe that a building must have utility. But another part of me is interested in big forms, big architectural forms. Even when I was designing my stainless steel furniture, I also saw each one as an object—a piece of sculpture in space. In fact, what really interested me was that they were a free form. I don't see that the two—function and sculpture—must exclude each other."

Any account of Breuer's evolution must obviously begin with his early Bauhaus days. At eighteen, at the end of the First World War, he had left the provincial Hungarian town of Pécs and had come to Vienna to study sculpture. A brief visit to the art academy, where students were copying plaster casts, convinced him he should look elsewhere. He proceeded to apprentice himself to a furniture maker, a venture which ended disastrously when he clumsily dented a hand plane by hammering on its edge and was so ashamed he never returned.

When a fellow Hungarian told him that the Bauhaus, which Walter Gropius had just opened in Weimar, proposed to combine practical crafts with art and architecture, Breuer hurried there to become one of the first students. From the beginning, the Bauhaus existed in controlled chaos; that it evolved in any coherent fashion is due to the immense patience, tolerance, and iron will of Gropius. For instance, the carpentry shop in which Breuer found himself was then in its headiest craft stage, with students exhorted to "sing like the soldier, sing like the slaves" as they hand-rubbed furniture. Breuer's first object, a carved Magyar chair, is almost a parody on the times, an effort—and happily his last—to see "how far can you go in the romantic, handcraft tradition." But so successful were his succeeding designs that at the age of twenty-two he was put in charge of the carpentry shop. He used his first wages to buy the two most modern objects he could think of: a typewriter and a bicycle.

It was as if Breuer had leapt from the nineteenth to the twentieth century in a matter of months. He was proud, for instance, that he flew in an airplane before he rode in an automobile, and did both before he used the telephone. Anything bearing the mark of advanced technology struck him as well-nigh miraculous. When a friend, while admiring his bicycle, told Breuer that he should see the making of bicycle handle bars—"They bend them just like spaghetti"—Breuer seized on the idea for furniture design. Working with an occasionally inebriated local plumber, Breuer constructed the first nickel-plated chair,

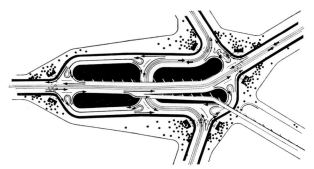

Breuer's design for Berlin's Potsdamer Platz called for a two-level, cloverleaf traffic interchange.

A 1936 project for a "Civic Center of the Future" forecast Breuer's later designs, with its acoustically formed theatre, trifoil pavilions, Y-shaped office buildings, and its shopping center with set-back ramps.

using lightweight twenty-millimeter cold-drawn tubing with welded joints. It was an instant success; Wassily Kandinsky, for whom Breuer named the chair, pronounced it "*Wunderbar!*" Breuer himself recalls, "I considered such polished and curved lines not only symbolic of our modern technology, but actually technology itself."

When the Bauhaus moved to Dessau in 1925, Gropius commissioned Breuer to furnish the school's new quarters; the interiors, including Breuer's furniture, were endlessly photographed, and his reputation as a brilliant young designer was assured. The Bauhaus, under the direction of younger masters such as Albers, Moholy-Nagy, and Breuer, was then rapidly shifting from a craft orientation to technology and mass production. In some ways, however, the Bauhaus under Gropius was not altogether satisfactory. Architecture was present in the curriculum more as a presiding goddess than as an actual subject; what building designs the school produced were strictly the products of Gropius's own office. For Breuer, whose ambitions by now went far beyond furnishing interiors, this was particularly galling.

In 1928 he decided to strike out on his own, opening his first office in Berlin. As a stake, he took with him the design for what became his most famous single piece of furniture, the 1928 cantilever chair. Because heavier tubing was now available, he was able to make a chair from one continuous, resilient tube. Combined with this most modern of materials, however, were two of the oldest: bentwood frames and straw caning, a combination of advanced technology and traditional materials that was soon to evidence itself in his architecture.

For Breuer, contrast is what gives vitality and zest to life. He has been inspired by the traditional masonry struc-

tures of Hungary, and at the same time he admires the machined aesthetic of the airplane; he prefers both air conditioning *and* the fireplace. By preference he places polished surface next to rough, and inserts plate glass directly into fieldstone masonry. For Breuer, significantly, one of the great lessons of the Parthenon is the fact that the temple's completely ordered, man-made forms are set in direct juxtaposition to the rough, untouched rock of the surrounding Acropolis.

This strong play of contrasts is disciplined by his bold geometry, his meticulous attention to plan and function. The shift from major conception to the working out of small details is not always successful; there is occasionally the sense that an inordinate amount of energy has gone into solving the minutiae of a problem. Walls are geometrically balanced out into space for no other purpose than to screen a service entrance, or a bridge walk has been allowed to break up what otherwise would have been a major space.

But as a creator of architectural forms, Breuer has proved himself to be both a major innovator and a stubborn one. An early summary of his concepts is a project, "Civic Center of the Future," which he, along with F. R. S. Yorke, presented in London in 1936 on the eve of his departure for the United States. It is a veritable catalogue of forms that Breuer had evolved, including a 1928 study for cloverleaf passenger-car interchange, an acoustically shaped theater, the Y-shaped office structures (later used for the UNESCO headquarters in Paris), trifoil pavilions (later erected in Argentina and Rotterdam), and a hollow-square shopping center whose set-back ramps are forerunners of the Whitney Museum's massive cantilevered façade.

Breuer continued to expound and develop these ideas

at the Harvard school of design, where he taught from 1937 to 1946. Along with Gropius, who became the director of the school, he was responsible for teaching the principles of the modern movement to a whole generation of Harvard graduate students, among them at least a dozen of the leading architects of today. At the time, the two architects, both refugees from Nazi Germany, were practically synonymous. Outside the classroom, Gropius and Breuer were also in partnership, designing in 1938 their first house, for the Haggerty family, in Cohasset, south of Boston.

Today, nearly thirty years later, it is clear that certain elements of the Haggerty house were Breuer's—notably the geometric fieldstone walls and the elegant outdoor stairway. But it was not until Breuer built his own house in Lincoln, Massachusetts, that his students began to understand his principles in action. There was the surprise of his copious use of fieldstone masonry, as well as such altogether American features as a screened porch, a duplex interior, and a massive end wall with a fireplace.

His structural innovations at first were largely worked out in terms of wood construction. A chance trip through New England in the wake of the 1938 hurricane forcefully demonstrated to him the remarkable strength of the traditional frame house; the roads were blocked with hundred-year-old elms snapped off at the trunk, yet the houses had survived the storm undamaged. He proceeded to figure out how the nailed-together American balloon-frame could be made to extend out into space as a series of trusses.

Breuer's summer cottage, erected near one of the ponds of Wellfleet on Cape Cod, also contained many lessons. He had taken a sloping, uneven site, and by setting the house on posts, had raised the whole structure aloft without disturbing the ground cover. Projecting from the house was a balcony supported by marine cables. The effect from within was intoxicating, as if one were floating out over the landscape.

Any Breuer house, in fact, can be studied with profit, either for its plan or its structural system and innovations. What is most evident is that Breuer has designed for living. From the very first he planned for family life: his kitchens are often observation posts, with views toward both playroom and living area; stone slabs, impervious to

The cantilevered Lecture Hall for the University Heights Campus of New York University contains two stepped auditoriums—one at left and the other at right. Breuer placed the hall on a steep, rocky slope between the laboratory building and the residence buildings. The bridge at far left leads to the Community Hall. Breuer designed all four buildings and, for the Lecture Hall, used textured concrete and faceted surfaces to emphasize its dramatic cantilevered construction.

The walls of the Whitney Museum (above) are pierced in random fashion by irregular polygon windows that give gallery-goers relief from the claustrophobia of closed gallery walls and serve also as architectural adornments. Breuer's fascination with the play of geometrical forms in space sometimes leads him to bizarre extremes. The fieldstone walls of this Massachusetts house (below) illustrate the effort—and rock—he was willing to expend to mask a service area.

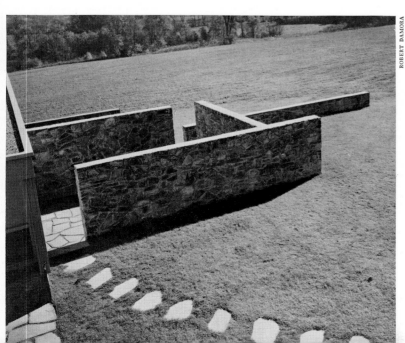

snow and mud, appear inside front doors. Most of all, the needs of both adults and children are recognized, and the result is often a twin-center house, with each age group given its own area.

To me, his most successful solutions have utilized a hillside site, for here he can create a floating structure on columns, providing at the lower, downhill side direct and immediate contact with nature—as close as the other side of the glass. However, Breuer's current house, in New Canaan, Connecticut—the fourth he has built for himself in the United States—is on one level and is constructed of great fieldstone walls, alternating with floor-to-ceiling glass which overlooks nearby fields and woods.

"Architecture has to create forms which stand repetition," Breuer says. But in his own work, he believes that each building should help to advance the state of building technology: "As far as I am concerned, this experimentation is the controlling factor in the most disciplined work—or it should be. The result may be commonplace, but in the process of conception, it was at least attempted."

One problem, on which he has focused with almost ferocious intensity, is the need to protect large expanses of glass from glare and heat. It is a problem which most architects today would probably solve by a combination of interior Venetian blinds and huge air-conditioning plants. But until a mechanical solution was found, the problem was critical if glass was to be fully utilized.

Finding ways to deal with sunlight obsessed Breuer from his 1931 "House for a Sportsman" to his UNESCO headquarters, completed in 1958. In the latter, the Y-shaped secretariat has a façade virtually ablaze with exterior solar-glass panels, louvers, and overhangs. The effect is almost baroque, a shimmering façade-in-depth in which a multiplicity of shading devices have been raised to the level of architectural ornament. But one wonders if all the effort expended on them was worth it, since UNESCO is one of the last major structures likely to be completed on a budget so restricted that air conditioning cannot be included.

Increasingly, in the past decade, Breuer has been experimenting with the potentialities of reinforced concrete, in large part as a result of his collaboration with the Italian engineer Pier Luigi Nervi on the UNESCO building. Breuer, of course, had designed concrete buildings almost from the beginning and has described the material enthusiastically as "the completely plastic medium"—the means to design "a sculpture with a function." And in Nervi he found a kindred spirit for whom structure is "both a principle and a passion," and who is a past master in the art of expressing it in concrete.

Borrowing a term from Frank Lloyd Wright, Breuer describes Nervi's analysis of structural systems as "organic": "This means a flow as real as the continuous strain starting at the shoulder, moving through the upper and lower arm, into the grip of the hand, fingers, and thumb. This is the real world of Nervi, the continuous stresses, branching out from support to girders, dividing into ribs and into the very fibers of the structure, only to combine again into ribs and columns."

This is also, clearly, the world of Breuer today. There are few sculptural masses more impressive in modern architecture than his colossally cantilevered Lecture Hall for New York University's Bronx campus or the muscular, branched columns that support the IBM Research Center at La Gaude, above the French Riviera. In many ways the finest expression of Breuer's mastery of reinforced concrete is his one-hundred-foot-tall bell banner, designed for St. John's Abbey in Collegeville, Minnesota. This ecclesiastical and university complex, I feel, would long ago have received acclaim as one of the outstanding architectural monuments in the United States were it not so isolated from the paths normally traveled by the critics.

It was precisely these later works which attracted the building committee of the Whitney Museum when they chose Breuer to design their new museum. I recall sitting outdoors with Breuer over late-afternoon cocktails on Cape Cod soon after the commission was announced. Several leading members of the Provincetown summer artists' community were present, including Robert Motherwell and Helen Frankenthaler. Breuer began to probe for ideas; what the artists wanted was something very similar to the environment of their own studios.

This Breuer has given them at the Whitney, including a main gallery seventeen and a half feet high, which is one of the grandest new exhibition areas yet created for modern art. Breuer could not resist adding a piece of "sculpture" of his own to this splendid space: the large, trapezoidal window that dominates the front of the gallery. This exuberant gesture is justified by Breuer in terms of the need to establish visual contact with the street from within an air-conditioned museum for which windows are actually obsolete. The final result, however, transcends any such functional requirements.

As for the exterior of the museum, Breuer was on his own. "It is easier to say first what it should *not* look like," he confessed. "It should not look like a business or office building, nor should it look like a place of light entertainment. Its form and its material should have identity and weight in the midst of the dynamic jungle of our colorful city. It should be an independent and self-reliant unit, exposed to history, and at the same time it should have a visual connection to the street." The projecting façade was chosen in part, as he admits, because it is "a form I happen to like." (It was originally proposed in a 1928 hospital design and again in his 1936 "Civic Center

Stairways and fireplaces have always been siezed upon by Breuer as occasions for sculptural effects. For the UNESCO Headquarters in Paris, the requirement for a fire stair (above) was used with almost baroque effect to create a play of concrete forms and ribbonlike metal railings. For the Clark house, in Orange, Connecticut, Breuer designed a freestanding fireplace of brick (below) that becomes a cubist exercise in its virtuoso balance of massive forms and voids.

BEN SCHNALL

Breuer's proposed design for the Franklin D. Roosevelt Memorial in Washington, D.C. (left), was composed of a series of triangular granite slabs encompassing a monolithic cube on which an image of FDR was to be engraved. Though approved by the Memorial Commission and the Roosevelt family, it was rejected by the Washington Fine Arts Commission.

Breuer was able to set his own stage for the dramatic bell banner at St. John's Benedictine Abbey in Minnesota. Borne aloft on parabolic arches, the concrete slab directly in front of the church (opposite) takes the place of a steeple or a campanile as a platform for the church bells of the monastery.

of the Future.") What made it particularly apt for the Whitney's small corner lot was that it would allow an exposed sculpture garden at the base at the same time that it provided increased gallery space on the upper floors.

No functional guidelines were offered Breuer when he was commissioned last year to design the Franklin Delano Roosevelt Memorial. The problem was complicated by the memorial's long and troubled history—one that was to doom Breuer's design, too, as it happened. Although the previous design (dubbed "instant Stonehenge" by its critics) won the approval of the capital's Fine Arts Commission, it was rejected by the Roosevelt family. The Memorial Commission this time interviewed five leading architects before unanimously settling on Breuer. It gave its enthusiastic endorsement to his design, which also won the approval of the Roosevelts—only to be turned down by the Fine Arts Commission. Even at this late date, modern architecture still has its battles to win. The site picked for the FDR Memorial is midway on an axis between the Jefferson and Lincoln memorials, and apparently the Fine Arts Commission expected something similar to those Greco-Roman mausoleums.

Breuer, as might be expected, took a different approach. He attempted to indicate both the grandeur of Roosevelt's concepts and their impact on the lives of the common man. To achieve this, Breuer went back to basic principles. "The art of architectural composition," as he has said, "lies in asembling simple, elemental forms to arrive at basic solutions." The form he finally found most satisfactory was a seven-point vortex that, viewed from

the air, looks like a turbine with mighty granite triangles —sixty feet high at the apex—as the blades. At the center was to be a gigantic monolithic cube, which was to have engraved on its surface in the manner of a photographic halftone, a picture of FDR; to evoke something of his personality, the design called for recordings of his more famous addresses and fireside chats, delivered at normal voice level. The result was impressive, monumental, and yet a place, as Breuer put it, "to relax, to stroll, to sit around, to contemplate—in the shadow of the trees and stone walls, or in the sun."

It is a pity the memorial will never be built. But the disappointment did not long deter Breuer. "To build . . . is not to play a role, not to take a vote, not to give an opinion," Breuer believes. "It is a passion, basic as the bread we eat." It is also the agony of the search, the endless balancing of function, form, and structural system, the never-ending pursuit of a solution in terms of the technology and art of our time. It has lead him to explore the whole spectrum, from gleaming, tensile steel to monolithic banners of reinforced concrete. One of the pioneer moderns, Breuer has created solutions that have become part of the syntax of our time, and at the same time, along with Frank Lloyd Wright, Mies van der Rohe, and Le Corbusier, he has given us the landmarks by which we recognize ourselves. For a career still far from over, this is no mean achievement.

Cranston Jones, a senior editor of Time *in charge of the magazine's art section, is the author of three books on architectural subjects, including one on Marcel Breuer.*

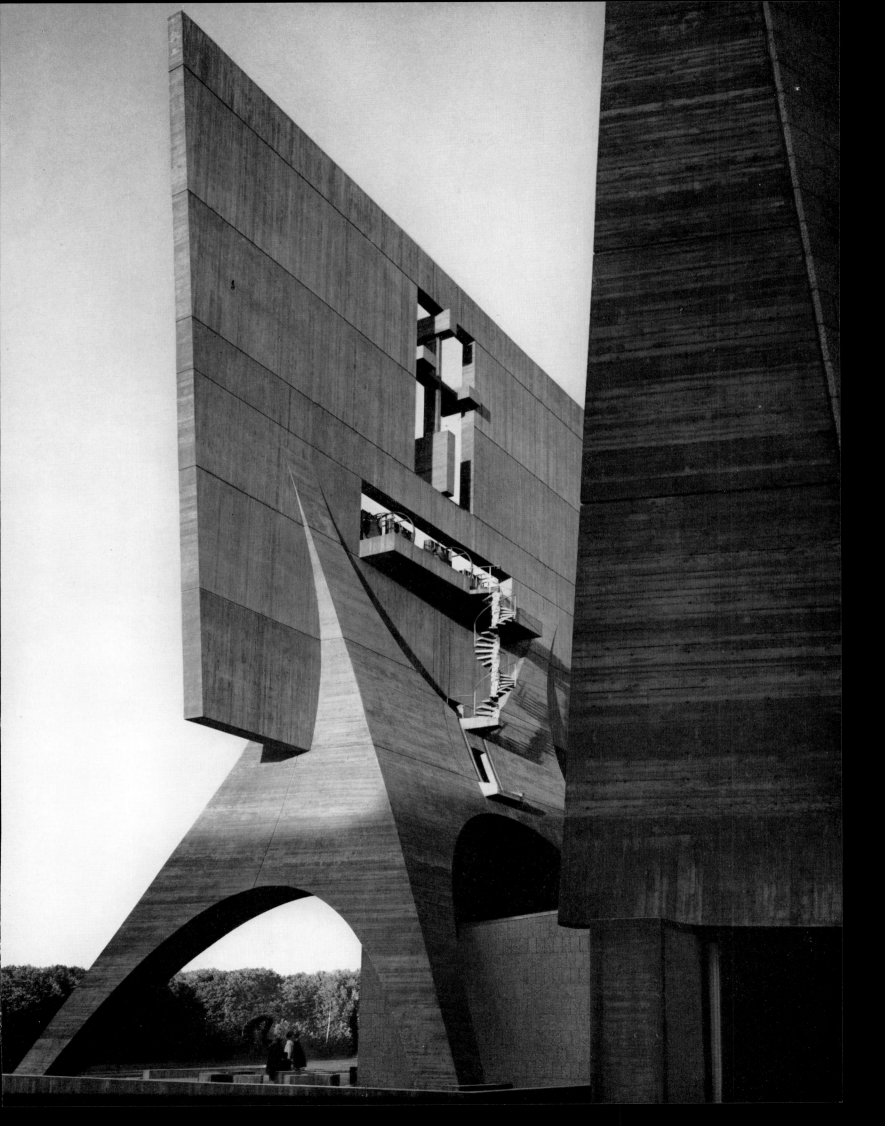

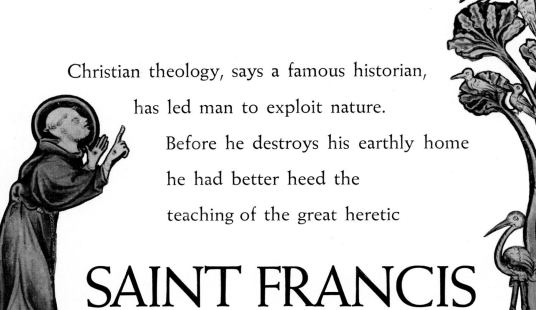

Christian theology, says a famous historian,
has led man to exploit nature.
Before he destroys his earthly home
he had better heed the
teaching of the great heretic

SAINT FRANCIS AND THE ECOLOGIC BACKLASH

A conversation with Aldous Huxley not infrequently put one at the receiving end of an unforgettable monologue. About a year before his lamented death he was discoursing on a favorite topic: man's unnatural treatment of nature and its sad results. To illustrate his point he told how, during the previous summer, he had returned to a little valley in England where he had spent many happy months as a child. Once it had been composed of delightful grassy glades; now it was becoming overgrown with unsightly brush because the rabbits that formerly kept such growth under control had largely succumbed to a disease, myxomatosis, that was deliberately introduced by the local farmers to reduce the rabbits' destruction of crops. Being something of a Philistine, I could be silent no longer, even in the interests of great rhetoric. I interrupted to point out that the rabbit itself had been brought as a domestic animal to England in 1176, presumably to improve the protein diet of the peasantry.

All forms of life modify their contexts. Ever since man became a numerous species he has affected his environment notably. The hypothesis that his fire-drive method of hunting created the world's great grasslands and helped to exterminate the monster mammals of the Pleistocene from much of the globe is plausible, if not proved. For six millenniums at least, the banks of the Lower Nile have

This article is adapted from the keynote address delivered by the author at the annual meeting of the American Association for the Advancement of Science. Professor White is a distinguished medieval historian as well as a former president of Mills College. He is now on the faculty of the University of California at Los Angeles.

been an artifact rather than the swampy African jungle that nature, apart from man, would have made them. The Aswan Dam, flooding nearly two thousand square miles, is only the latest stage in a long process. In many regions terracing or irrigation, overgrazing, the cutting of forests by Romans to build ships to fight Carthaginians or by Crusaders to solve the logistics problems of their expeditions, have profoundly changed some ecologies. Observation that the French landscape falls into two basic types, the open fields of the north and the *bocage* of the south and west, inspired Marc Bloch to undertake his classic study of medieval agricultural methods. Quite unintentionally, changes in human ways often affect nonhuman nature. It has been noted, for example, that the advent of the automobile eliminated the huge flocks of sparrows that once fed on the horse manure littering every street.

The history of ecologic change is

By LYNN WHITE, JR.

still so rudimentary that we know little about what really happened, or what the results were. The extinction of the European aurochs as late as 1627 would seem to have been a simple case of overenthusiastic hunting. On more intricate matters it often is impossible to find solid information. For a thousand years or more the Frisians and Hollanders have been pushing back the North Sea, and the process is culminating in our own time in the reclamation of the Zuider Zee. What, if any, species of animals, birds, fish, shore life, or plants have died out in the process? In their epic combat with Neptune have the Netherlanders over-looked ecologic values in such a way that the quality of human life in the Netherlands has suffered? I cannot discover that the questions have ever been asked, much less answered.

People, then, have often been a dynamic element in their own environment, but in the present state of historical scholarship we usually do not know precisely when, where, or with what effects man-induced changes came. As we enter the last third of the twentieth century, however, concern for the problem of ecologic backlash is mounting feverishly. Natural science, conceived as the effort to understand the nature of things, had flourished in several eras and among several peoples. Similarly there had been an age-old accumulation of technological skills, sometimes growing rapidly, sometimes slowly. But it was not until about four generations ago that western Europe and North America arranged a marriage between science and technology, a union of the theoretical and the empirical approaches to our natural environment. The emergence in widespread practice of the Baconian creed that scientific knowledge means technological power over nature can scarcely be dated before about 1850, except in the chemical industries,

where it was anticipated in the eighteenth century. Its acceptance as a normal pattern of action may mark the greatest event in human history—and perhaps in nonhuman terrestrial history as well—since the invention of agriculture.

Almost at once the new situation forced the crystallization of the novel concept of ecology; indeed, the word "ecology" first appeared in the English language in 1873. Today, less than a century later, the impact of our race upon the environment has so increased in force that it has changed in essence. When the first cannons were fired, in the early fourteenth century, they affected ecology by sending workers scrambling to the forests and mountains for more potash, sulfur, iron ore, and charcoal, with some resulting erosion and deforestation. Hydrogen bombs are of a different order: a war fought with them might alter the genetics of all life on this planet. By 1285 London had a smog problem arising from the burning of soft coal, but our present combustion of fossil fuels threatens to change the chemistry of the globe's atmosphere as a whole, with consequences that we are only beginning to guess. With the population explosion, the carcinoma of planless urbanism, the now geological deposits of sewage and garbage, surely no creature other than man has ever managed to foul its nest in such short order.

There are many calls to action, but specific proposals, however worthy as individual items, seem too partial, palliative, negative. Of course the simplest solution to any suspect change is to stop it or, better yet, to revert to a romanticized past: make those ugly gasoline stations look like Anne Hathaway's cottage or (in the Far West) like ghost-town saloons. The "wilderness area" mentality invariably advocates deep-freezing an ecology, whether San Gimignano or the High

Sierra, as it was before the first Kleenex was dropped. But neither atavism nor prettification will cope with the ecologic crisis of our time.

What shall we do? No one yet knows. Unless we think about fundamentals, our measures may produce new backlashes more serious than those they are designed to remedy.

As a beginning we should try to clarify our thinking by looking, in some historical depth, at the presuppositions that underlie modern technology and science. Science was traditionally aristocratic, speculative, intellectual, in intent; technology was lower class, empirical, action oriented. The quite sudden fusion of these two, toward the middle of the nineteenth century, is surely related to the slightly prior and contemporary democratic revolutions which, by reducing social barriers, tended to assert a functional unity of brain and hand. Our ecologic crisis is the product of an emerging, entirely novel, democratic culture. The issue is whether a democratized world can survive its own implications. Presumably it cannot unless we rethink our axioms.

Modern science and technology have their roots in the Middle Ages

Both modern technology and modern science are distinctively Occidental. Our technology has absorbed elements from all over the world, notably from China; yet everywhere today, whether in Japan or in Nigeria, successful technology is Western. Our science is heir to all the sciences of the past, especially perhaps to the work of the great Islamic scientists of the Middle Ages who so often outdid the ancient Greeks in skill and perspicacity: al-Rāzī in medicine, for example; or ibn-al-Haytham in optics. Indeed, not a few works of such geniuses seem to have vanished in the original Arabic and to survive only in medieval Latin translations that helped to lay the foundations for later Western developments. Today, around the globe, all significant science is Western in style and method.

Two further facts are less well recognized because they result from quite recent historical scholarship. The leadership of the West, both in technology and in science, is far older than the so-called Scientific Revolution of the seventeenth century or the so-called Industrial Revolution of the eighteenth century. These terms are in fact outmoded and obscure the true nature of what they try to describe—significant stages in two long and separate developments. By A.D. 1000 at the latest—and perhaps, feebly, for two hundred years earlier—the West began to apply water power to industrial processes other than the milling of grain. This was followed in the late twelfth century by the harnessing of wind power. From simple beginnings, but with remarkable consistency of style, the West rapidly expanded its skills in the development of power machinery, labor-saving devices, and automation. Those who doubt should contemplate that most monumental achievement in the history of automation: the weight-driven mechanical clock, which appeared in two forms in the early fourteenth century. Not in craftsmanship, but in basic technological capacity, the Latin West of the later Middle Ages far outstripped the elaborate, sophisticated, and aesthetically magnificent cultures of Byzantium and Islam. In 1444 a great Greek ecclesiastic, Bessarion, who had gone to Italy, wrote a letter to a prince in Greece. He was amazed by the superiority of Western ships, arms, textiles, glass.

But above all he was astonished by the spectacle of water wheels sawing timbers and pumping the bellows of blast furnaces. Clearly, he had seen nothing of the sort in the Near East.

By the end of the fifteenth century the technological superiority of Europe was such that its small, mutually hostile nations could spill out over all the rest of the world, conquering, looting, and colonizing. The symbol of this technological superiority is the fact that Portugal, one of the weakest states of the Occident, was able to become, and to remain for a century, mistress of the East Indies. And we must remember that the technology **of Vasco da Gama and Albuquerque** was based on pure empiricism, drawing remarkably little support or inspiration from science.

In the present-day vernacular understanding, modern science is supposed to have begun in 1543, when both Copernicus and Vesalius published their great works. It is no derogation of their accomplishments, however, to point out that such structures as the *De Revolutionibus* and the *Fabrica* do not appear overnight. The distinctive Western tradition of science, in fact, began in the late eleventh century with a massive movement of translation of Arabic and Greek scientific works into Latin. A few notable books—Theophrastus, for one—escaped the West's avid new appetite for science, but within less than two hundred years, in effect the entire corpus of Greek and Moslem science was available in Latin and was being eagerly read and criticized in the new European universities. Out of criticism arose new observation, speculation, and increasing distrust of ancient authorities. By the late thirteenth century Europe had seized global scientific leadership from the faltering hands of Islam. It would be as absurd to deny the profound originality of Newton, Galileo, or Copernicus as

to deny that of the fourteenth-century scholastic scientists like Buridan or Oresme, on whose work they built. Before the eleventh century, science scarcely existed in the Latin West, even in Roman times. From the eleventh century onward, the scientific sector of Occidental culture has increased in a steady crescendo.

Since both our technological and our scientific movements got their start, acquired their character, and achieved world dominance in the Middle Ages, it would seem that we cannot understand their nature or their present impact upon ecology without examining fundamental medieval assumptions and developments.

The European peasant's plow broke the sod— and broke man's dependence on nature

Until recently, agriculture has been the chief occupation even in "advanced" societies; hence, any change in methods of tillage has much importance. Early plows, drawn by two oxen, did not normally turn the sod but merely scratched it. Thus, cross-plowing was needed and fields tended to be squarish. In the fairly light soils and semiarid climates of the Near East and Mediterranean, this worked well. But such a plow was inappropriate to the wet climate and often sticky soils of northern Europe. By the latter part of the seventh century, however, following obscure beginnings, certain northern peasants were using an entirely new kind of plow, equipped with a vertical knife to cut the line of the furrow, a horizontal share to slice under the sod, a moldboard to turn it over. The friction of this plow against the soil was so great that it normally required not two but eight oxen. It attacked the land with such violence that cross-plowing was not needed, and fields tended to be shaped in long strips.

In the days of the scratch plow, fields were distributed generally in units capable of supporting a single family. Subsistence farming was the presupposition. But no peasant owned eight oxen; to use the new and more efficient plow, peasants pooled their oxen to form large plow teams, originally receiving (it would appear) plowed strips in proportion to their contribution. Thus, distribution of land was no longer based on the needs of a family but rather on the capacity of a power machine to till the earth. Man's relation to the soil was profoundly changed. Formerly man had been part of nature; now he was the exploiter of nature. Nowhere else in the world did farmers develop any analogous agricultural implement. Is it coincidence that modern technology, with its ruthlessness toward nature, has so largely been produced by descendants of these peasants of northern Europe?

This same exploitive attitude appears slightly before A.D. 830 in Western illustrated calendars. In older calendars the months were shown as passive personifications. The new Frankish calendars, which set the style for the Middle Ages, are very different: they show men coercing the world around them—plowing, harvesting, chopping trees, butchering pigs. Man and nature are two things, and man is master.

These novelties seem to be in harmony with larger intellectual patterns. The attitude of people toward their ecology depends on what they think about themselves in relation to things around them. Human ecology is deeply conditioned by beliefs about our nature and destiny—that is, by religion. To Western eyes this is very evident in, say, India or Ceylon. It is equally true of ourselves and of our medieval ancestors.

The victory of Christianity over paganism has been the greatest psychic revolution in the history of our culture. It has become fashionable today to say that, for better or worse, we live in "the post-Christian age." Certainly the forms of our thinking and language have largely ceased to be Christian, but to my eye the substance often remains amazingly akin to that of the past. Our daily habits of action, for example, are dominated by an implicit faith in perpetual progress that was unknown either to Greco-Roman antiquity or to the Orient. It is rooted in, and is indefensible apart from, Judaeo-Christian teleology. The fact that Communists share it merely helps to show what can be demonstrated on many other grounds: that Marxism, like Islamism, is a Judaeo-Christian heresy. We continue today to live as we have lived for about seventeen hundred years, largely in a context of Christian axioms.

Christianity taught that God created all of nature for man's sole benefit

While many of the world's mythologies provide stories of creation, Greco-Roman mythology was singularly incoherent in this respect. Like Aristotle, the intellectuals of the ancient West denied that the visible world had had a beginning. Indeed, the idea of a beginning was impossible in the framework of their cyclical notion of time. In sharp contrast, Christianity inherited from Judaism not only a concept of time as non-repetitive and linear but also a striking story of creation. By gradual stages a loving and all-powerful God had created light and darkness, the heavenly bodies, the earth and all its plants, animals, birds, and fishes. Finally, God had created Adam and as an afterthought, Eve, to keep man from being lonely. Man named all the animals, thus establishing his dominance over them. God had planned all of this explicitly for man's benefit and rule: no item in the physical creation had any purpose save to serve man's purposes. And although man's body is made of clay, he is not simply part of nature: he is made in God's image.

Especially in its Western form, Christianity is the most anthropocentric religion the world has seen. As early as the second century both Tertullian and Saint Irenaeus of Lyons were insisting that when God shaped Adam he was foreshadowing the image of the incarnate Christ, the Second Adam. Man shares, in great measure, God's transcendence of nature. Christianity, in absolute contrast to ancient paganism and Asia's religions (except perhaps Zoroastrianism), not only established a dualism of man and nature but also insisted that it is God's will that man exploit nature for his own ends.

At the level of the common people this worked out in an interesting way. In antiquity every tree, every spring, every stream, every hill, had its own *genius loci*, its guardian spirit. These spirits were accessible to men, but were very unlike men. Before one cut a tree, mined a mountain, or dammed a brook, it was important to placate the spirit in charge of that particular situation, and to keep it placated. By destroying pagan animism, Christianity made it possible to exploit nature in a mood of indifference to the feelings of natural objects.

It is often said that for animism the Church substituted the cult of saints. True; but the cult of saints is functionally quite different from animism. The saint is not *in* natural objects; he may have special shrines, but his citizenship is in heaven. Moreover, a saint is entirely a man; he can be approached in human terms. In addition to saints, Christianity of course also had angels and demons inherited from Judaism and perhaps, at one remove, from Zoroastrianism. But these were all as mobile as the saints themselves. The spirits *in* natural objects, which formerly had protected nature from man, evaporated. Man's effective monopoly of spirit in this world was confirmed, and the old inhibitions to the exploitation of nature crumbled.

When one speaks in such sweeping terms, a note of caution is in order. Christianity is a complex faith, and its consequences differ in differing contexts. What I have said may well apply to the medieval West, where in fact technology made spectacular advances. But the Greek East, a highly civilized realm of equal Christian devotion, seems to have produced no marked technological innovation after the late seventh century, when Greek fire was invented. The key to the contrast may perhaps be found in a difference in the tonality of piety and thought that students of comparative theology find between the Greek and the Latin churches. The Greeks believed that sin was intellectual blindness, and that salvation was found in illumination, orthodoxy—that is, clear thinking. The Latins, on the other hand, felt that sin was moral evil, and that salvation was to be found in right conduct. The implications of Christianity for the conquest of nature would emerge more easily in the Western atmosphere.

The Christian dogma of creation, which is found in the first clause of all the creeds, has another meaning for our comprehension of today's ecologic crisis. By revelation, God had given man the Bible, the Book of Scripture. But since God had made

nature, nature must also reveal the divine mentality. The religious study of nature for the better understanding of God was known as natural theology. In the early Church, and always in the Greek East, nature was conceived primarily as a symbolic system through which God speaks to men: the ant is a sermon to sluggards; rising flames are the symbol of the soul's aspiration. This view of nature was essentially artistic rather than scientific. Although Byzantium preserved and copied great numbers of ancient Greek scientific texts, science as we conceive it could scarcely flourish in such an *ambiance*.

However, by the early thirteenth century, natural theology in the Latin West was following a very different bent. It was ceasing to be the decoding of the physical symbols of God's communication with man and was becoming the effort to understand God's mind by discovering how His creation operates. The rainbow was no longer simply a symbol of hope, first sent to Noah after the Deluge; Robert Grosseteste, Friar Roger Bacon, and Theodoric of Freiberg produced startlingly sophisticated work on the optics of the rainbow, but they did it as a venture in religious understanding. From the thirteenth century onward, up to and including Leibnitz and Newton, every major scientist in effect explained his motivations in religious terms. Indeed, if Galileo had not been so expert an amateur theologian, he would have got into far less trouble: the professionals resented his intrusion. And Newton seems to have regarded himself more as a theologian than as a scientist. It was not until the late eighteenth century that the hypothesis of God became unnecessary to many scientists.

It is often hard for the historian to judge, when men explain why they are doing what they want to do, whether they are offering real reasons

or merely culturally acceptable reasons. The consistency with which scientists during the long formative centuries of Western science said that the task and the reward of the scientist was "to think God's thoughts after him" leads one to believe that this was their real motivation. If so, then modern Western science was cast in a matrix of Christian theology. The dynamism of religious devotion, shaped by the Judaeo-Christian dogma of creation, gave it impetus.

"I propose Francis as a patron saint for ecologists"

We would seem to be headed toward conclusions unpalatable to many Christians. Since both "science" and "technology" are blessed words in our contemporary vocabulary, some may be happy about the notions, first, that modern science, viewed historically, is an extrapolation of natural theology and, second, that modern technology is at least partly to be explained as an Occidental, voluntarist realization of the Christian dogma of man's transcendence of, and rightful mastery over, nature. But, as we now recognize, a little more than a century ago science and technology—hitherto quite separate activities—joined to give mankind powers which, to judge by many of the ecologic effects, are out of control. If so, Christianity bears a huge burden of guilt.

I personally doubt that disastrous ecologic backlash can be avoided simply by applying to our problems more science and more technology. Our science and technology have grown out of Christian attitudes toward man's relation to nature that are almost universally held not only by Christians and neo-Christians but also by those who fondly regard themselves as post-Christians. Despite Copernicus, all the cosmos rotates around our little globe. Despite Darwin, we are *not*, in our hearts, part of the natural process. We are superior to nature, contemptuous of it, willing to use it for our slightest whim. The newly elected Governor of California, like myself a churchman but less troubled than I, spoke for the Christian tradition when he allegedly said, "when you've seen one redwood tree, you've seen them all." To a Christian a tree can be no more than a physical fact. The whole concept of the sacred grove is alien to Christianity and to the ethos of the West. For nearly two millenniums Christian missionaries have been chopping down sacred groves, considering them idolatrous because they assume spirit in nature.

What we do about ecology depends on our ideas of the man–nature relationship. More science and more technology are not going to get us out of the present ecologic crisis until we find a new religion, or rethink our old one. The beatniks, who are the basic revolutionaries of our time, show a sound instinct in their affinity for Zen Buddhism, which conceives of the man–nature relationship as very nearly the mirror image of the Christian view. Zen, however, is as deeply conditioned by Asian history as Christianity is by the experience of the West, and I am dubious of Zen's viability among us.

Possibly we should ponder the greatest radical in Christian history since Christ: Saint Francis of Assisi. The prime miracle of Saint Francis is the fact that he did not end at the stake, as many of his left-wing followers did. He was so clearly heretical that a general of the Franciscan order, Saint Bonaventure, a great and perceptive Christian, tried to suppress the early accounts of Franciscanism. The key to an understanding of Francis is his belief in the virtue of humil-

ity—not merely for the individual but for man as a species. Francis tried to depose man from his rule over creation and to set up a democracy of all God's creatures. For him the ant is no longer simply a homily for the lazy, nor are flames a sign of the thrust of the soul toward union with God; now they are Brother Ant and Sister Fire, praising the Creator in their own ways, as Brother Man does in his.

Later commentators have said that Francis preached to the birds as a rebuke to men who would not listen. The records do not read so; he urged the little birds to praise God, and in spiritual ecstasy they flapped their wings and chirped rejoicing. Legends of saints, especially the Irish saints, had long told of their dealings with animals but always, I believe, to show their human dominance over creatures. With Francis it is different. The land around Gubbio in the Apennines was being ravaged by a fierce wolf. Saint Francis, says the legend, talked to the wolf and persuaded him of the error of his ways. The wolf repented, died in the odor of sanctity, and was buried in consecrated ground.

What Sir Steven Ruciman calls "the Franciscan doctrine of the animal soul" was quickly stamped out. Quite possibly it was in part inspired, consciously or unconsciously, by the belief in reincarnation held by the Cathar heretics who at that time abounded in Italy and Southern France, and who presumably had got it originally from India. It is significant that at just the same moment, about 1200, traces of metempsychosis are found also in western Judaism, in the Provençal *Cabbala*. But Francis held neither to transmigration of souls nor to pantheism. His view of nature and of man rested on a unique sort of pan-psychism of all things animate and inanimate, designed for the glorification of their transcendent Creator, who, in the ultimate gesture of cosmic

humility, assumed flesh, lay helpless in a manger, and died on a scaffold.

I am not suggesting that many contemporary Americans who are concerned about our ecologic crisis will be either able or willing to counsel with wolves or exhort birds. However, the present increasing disruption of the global environment is the product of a dynamic technology and science that were originating in the same Western medieval world against which Saint Francis was rebelling in so original a way. Their growth cannot be understood historically, apart from distinctive attitudes toward nature that are deeply grounded in Christian dogma. The fact that most people do not think of these attitudes as Christian is irrelevant. No new set of basic values has been accepted in our society to displace those of Christianity. Hence we shall continue to have a worsening ecologic crisis until we reject the Christian axiom that nature has no reason for existence save to serve man.

The greatest spiritual revolutionary in Western history, Saint Francis, proposed what he thought was an alternative Christian view of nature and man's relation to it: he tried to substitute the idea of the equality of all creatures, including man, for the idea of man's limitless rule over creation. He failed. Both our present science and our present technology are so tinctured with orthodox Christian arrogance toward nature that no solution for our ecologic crisis can be expected from them alone. Since the roots of our trouble are so largely religious, the remedy must also be essentially religious, whether we call it that or not. We must rethink and refeel our nature and destiny. The profoundly religious, but heretical, sense of the primitive Franciscans for the spiritual autonomy of all parts of nature may point a direction. I propose Francis as a patron saint for ecologists.

DAVID: The Napoleon of French Painting

Louis XVI, Robespierre, and Bonaparte were united in admiration of one man: Jacques Louis David. His heroic style, suppressing passion beneath a hard, chilly surface, made him the artistic dictator of France

Jacques Louis David emerges from most biographies as one of the least sympathetic personalities in the history of art, an impression not mitigated, for most people, by his painting, which they find as hard and as chilly as the man. Such a judgment—on both the man and his art—is superficial, but even if it were accurate, his life would remain an extraordinary combination of adventure tale and success story.

For anyone who can get through the layer of iciness, David is an endlessly fascinating painter. Though tradition has made him the archetype of the classicist who reduced antiquity to a kind of sterile purity, David is really only a pseudoclassicist whose variation of the formula was dominated by a combination of staggering realism and true romanticism. In his most frigid paintings an obsessive sensuality lies just beneath the surface. His nudes are at once adaptations of the idealized bodies of antique sculpture, carefully analyzed anatomical studies, and declarations of the allure of human nakedness that on occasion can amount to a revelation of concupiscence. David must have been a lustful man beneath his aesthetic puritanism, but he never thought of his idealized forms as a transmutation of sensual experience, as the original forms were with the Greeks. Only in an occasional portrait of a member of his family or a very close friend does he allow himself even a confession of tenderness. But his portraits are brilliant renderings of surface that become by second nature revelations of the personality of the sitter.

David's immaculate surface, the often enamel-like finish of his paintings, conceals preliminary stages that were as fresh and sensitive as the best rococo painting that he abominated. There are portions of unfinished works that might have been struck in by Gainsborough in his most delightful mood. David's last painting, of Mars and Venus, a love scene painted by an old man, is closer in spirit to his first master, Boucher, than to the rationalism into which he forced himself. And one portrait of Napoleon on horseback, *Napoleon Crossing the St. Bernard Pass*, is so full of wind and storm, with flying draperies and a rearing, wild-eyed steed, that it has become accepted as a protoromantic conception. During the century that followed David's death, three forces struggled for position in French art—classicism, romanticism, and realism. But their initial struggle took place in the art of a single painter, Jacques Louis David.

David began his career as a protégé of the state under the *ancien régime* of Louis XVI, continued it as a powerful figure in the Revolutionary government, went on from there to become the grand old man of French painting as a favorite of Napoleon's, and in the process redirected the course of French art at just the time when Paris was emerging as the art center of Europe. His single *faux pas* during his lifetime as a political chameleon—his enemies prefer the word turncoat—cost him the support of the Bourbons after the fall of Napoleon, but even so

Jailed after the fall of Robespierre in 1794, David painted this unfinished self-portrait in the tiny room where he was held in the Hôtel des Fermes. An artist who never worked without a model, he did the painting from his mirror image. The tumor which disfigured his cheek is shown in shadow.

By JOHN CANADAY

The Oath of the Horatii (1784) depicts an incident out of classical tradition in which three brothers of a patrician Roman family, pledging their lives for their country, receive swords from their father. One of the last official commissions of the ancien régime and a revolutionary departure in style, the painting was interpreted as a call for a return to ancient republican virtues. It is heroic in size as well: 11 feet high by 14 wide.

he holds a record for adaptive longevity under hazardous circumstances.

David was born in 1748. As if to make the story perfect, his origins were simple if not quite humble, and his early years were a struggle against a series of defeats that very nearly cost him his life by suicide. His father, a Parisian tradesman, died when David was nine, and he was brought up by two uncles, one a builder and the other an architect. It must have been during his boyhood that a tumor began to grow at one side of his mouth just above the upper lip. A self-portrait painted in 1794 shows it grown large enough to twist his face. It also impeded his speech. Little attention is paid to this disfigurement by David's biographers, which perhaps is just as well. It could easily be interpreted as the kind of harassing physical deformity that helps breed dictators, and David did become a dictator with a record that can be read to his disadvantage.

David was admitted to the Royal Academy as a student in 1766, when he was eighteen, and (we are told) was immediately attracted to the antique revival that was beginning to chasten the dainty flourishes of rococo style. When he became eligible to compete for the Prix de Rome he did so, and failed. He continued to compete, and to fail, year after year.

The Prix de Rome was (and remains) a fellowship awarded annually to a student of the Academy demonstrating, in the eyes of his teachers, exceptional talent. In David's time a test picture on an assigned subject was required as the nominal basis for the award, but the prize went regularly to the student who not only had demonstrated an acceptable talent but had been respectful of the standards of his teachers and had made himself personally engaging. At the Ecole des Beaux-Arts in Paris—the current school of the Academy—the Prix de Rome pictures, hanging together in a large room, are a history of the taste that dominated the Academy from year to year. Some of the winners are forgotten; some of the pictures are important early—almost juvenile—efforts by great names in the history of painting.

The Prix de Rome winner had every chance to succeed. He was immediately starred with the cachet of official approval. The only requirement during his stay in Rome was that he send back pictures at regular intervals for inspection (and to prove that he was working). If he was obedient and industrious, he returned to Paris an established artist and had no trouble receiving commissions from private patrons and the state.

Aside from his talent, David had few of the requirements for a Prix de Rome, but he was absolutely determined to win it. He hung on during successive failures that in themselves amounted to an informal blackball, managing to support himself with any work he could pick up. One godsend came through Fragonard, the reigning favorite of Parisian café society. He had begun the decorations for the Hôtel Guimard but soon abandoned them and turned the job over to David. To David's credit, he remembered this kindness after the Revolution, when he in his turn was up and Fragonard was down, by granting the old painter a sinecure with the state.

In 1772, at the low point of his life, David attempted suicide by means appropriate to a painter who was to establish a new stoic style: he locked himself in his room and resolved to starve to death. When he did not appear for several days, his fellow students broke in and rescued him. In 1773 David failed for the third time to win the Prix—although that was the year in which Fragonard's well-timed favor sustained him somewhat. Finally, in 1774, he competed again for the Prix and won—and the following year, at the age of twenty-seven, he was in Rome at last.

David was ready to dismiss the Academy altogether except for such help as it, alone, could give him. His failures to win the Prix had embittered him so deeply that he regarded his success as a victory over an enemy. A mature young man rather than a tag-end student (as the typical prize winner was), he plunged into Rome independently, determined to exhaust all it could offer him before his time there ran out.

He stayed five years, and began by gobbling up everything. The first paintings he sent back to Paris puzzled and disappointed his sponsors: they were dark and heavy pictures, inspired by the Bolognese painters, whose work David had discovered. It was a brief phase in his development, but can be read as significant in its rejection of the airiness and freshness of the rococo style, a first declaration of independence from the society that had rejected David for so long.

His sketchbooks from his first year are filled with notations of all kinds, from drawings made after details of baroque paintings to on-the-spot sketches of classical monuments. It was classical Rome that most fascinated him. His rejection of rococo artifice inspired him to a vision of heroic grandeur—not the opulent Rome of the Empire but Republican Rome with its severe moral code and its masculinity, a masculinity in utter contrast to the frills and laces of the regime in France. Even the classical revival that was under way at home, with the style now called Louis XVI—it could more appropriately be called Marie Antoinette—was a style of extreme delicacy in which classical motifs were adapted to the ideals of the boudoir and the drawing room.

When David returned to Paris, he was accepted in the usual way of a Prix de Rome man and had no trouble exhibiting in the Salon. He had not yet achieved the style of heroic severity that was to set him in opposition to the

In 1791 the Constituent Assembly commissioned David to immortalize the Oath of the Tennis Court. That was the moment when, in June, 1789, the Third Estate, locked out of its chamber by royal troops, met in an indoor tennis court and swore not to disband until a new constitution had been adopted—thus setting the stage for the Revolution. David's painting was never completed, though he had done most of the groundwork, including the oil portraits attached to nude bodies, right, and the wildly romanticized drawing above. The historian J. M. Thompson has described the latter: "... Bailly stands on a table, administering the oath .... carefully balanced groups of deputies stretch out their arms towards him. But Sieyès sits unmoved, as though pondering on the event ... Robespierre, the least demonstrative of men, strikes a dramatic attitude ... both hands upon his breast, as though (it was the artist's own explanation) he had two hearts beating for liberty."

David again turned to Roman history in The Lictors Bringing to Brutus the Bodies of his Sons (*above*), *based on the
story of the consul* (*seen brooding in the shadows, left*) *who
sentenced his own sons to death for conspiring to restore the
monarchy. The trio of grieving women in the detail opposite
has the granitic quality of a classical bas-relief, with only a
discarded sewing basket to give a feeling of home life. The
painting was exhibited in 1789, after the fall of the Bastille,
and the message that it imparted was not lost on its viewers.*

Academy's standards. His classicism was closely relatable
to that of Poussin, an Academy god, and David also
proved himself a supreme draftsman in the Academy's
tradition of the studio nude. Further, his celebrations of
the virtues of the ancient world appealed to the didactic
philosophers of the Age of Reason. There was as yet no
indication that the Academy was nurturing a murderous
rebel.

In his personal life David was also following a course
proper for a steady, ambitious young man. In 1782, two
years after his return from Rome, he married well, a bit
above his station. Marguerite Charlotte Pécoul was the
daughter of a contractor who was the king's superintendent of construction at the Louvre, a position that had
made him wealthy and carried with it certain connections
that could be helpful to a son-in-law. Marguerite was
seventeen when David married her and was perhaps a bit
of an ugly duckling; by the evidence of a portrait he did
of her in 1813, she never grew to be much of a swan,
even when decked out in the finest feathers that money
could buy. But over the years she proved herself to be
both spirited and faithful—spirited, once, when she left
David for what she considered a morally reprehensible
action on his part; faithful, when she returned to him because he was in trouble.

By 1784 David was well set. He had a rich wife and a
brilliant success in the Salon with a picture called *Andro-*

mache by the Body of Hector, which brought him election to the Academy. He had also received a royal commission from the Comte d'Angiviller (whose position as
general supervisor of all building under the king suggests
a connection with Marguerite's father) for the painting
that was to raise David from the position of successful
artist to that of sensational innovator.

D'Angiviller wanted a painting of the Oath of the
Horatii, based on a sketch David had done while watching a performance of Corneille's *Horace*. As David developed the idea, however, he worked out a composition that
was not taken from any of the play's tableaux. David began the painting in Paris (where he had a studio in the
Louvre, which was not yet a museum) but decided that
he could get into the spirit of it only in Rome. His father-
in-law provided the money for the trip, and this time
David returned to that inspiring city not as an aging
student but as an established painter, accompanied by his
wife, studio assistants, and servants; he returned as the
leader of a revolution in painting and was also declared a prophet of a revolution in government.

Whether or not the atmosphere of Rome contributed
to its conception, *The Oath of the Horatii* (see pages 50–
51) fulfilled David's classical ideal. He exhibited it first
in his studio in Rome, where it was a sensation. The
elements of the picture had been stripped down to the
minimum; every furbelow had been eliminated; the
brush was kept under rigid control—there was not a
flourish, not a squiggle of paint to mar the icy impersonal-
ity of its execution. The drawing was as hard as stone.
All fluidity, all spontaneity, all feminine elegance, had
given way to a determined philosophical masculinity.
The grieving women, who see their sons or husbands
perhaps going to their deaths, are given a secondary place,
subjugated to the tableau of father and sons dedicated to
the honor of country.

It was the style of the painting that created the sensation in Rome. In comparison with the sweet graces of the
current fashion it was as revolutionary as cubism would
be in the twentieth century. But in Paris the sensation was
doubled. *The Oath of the Horatii* was exhibited in the
Salon of 1785 and was interpreted not as a mere retelling
of Corneille's theme but as an allegorical comment on
the turmoil that was building up to revolution. It was
time, the picture seemed to say (although there is no
reason to think that David had any such interpretation
in mind), that France save herself from the degeneracy of
the old regime by returning to the ideals of firm repub-
licanism, no matter what sacrifices might be entailed. The
picture had been given an unfavorable position in the
Salon, no doubt because it challenged the accepted style
of the Academy, but the furor was so great that it was
rehung as the center of the show.

In the three portraits above, David's wife, Marguerite Charlotte, is flanked by their twin daughters, Emilie (left) and Pauline. Madame David was evidently more notable for her character and vivacity than for her looks. Free of a preconceived aesthetic and making no attempt to imitate the antique, these portraits are among David's most relaxed works. Some of the same naturalness is displayed in the View of the Luxembourg Gardens *(opposite). David's only landscape painting, it was executed from a window in the Luxembourg Palace where he was imprisoned in the autumn of 1794.*

The Revolution finally broke in 1789, as David was working on another exhibition picture illustrating a classical subject (the full title of the painting, page 54, is its description): "Brutus, First Consul, in his house after having condemned his two sons who had joined the Tarquins and conspired against Roman liberty. Lictors bring the corpses in order that he may give them burial." Again David was credited with Revolutionary sentiments presented in disguise, this time making Brutus the symbol of all Frenchmen who will make any personal sacrifice to protect French liberty. The particular targets were supposed to be the émigrés who had fled France in the crisis, with as much of their property as possible.

Early in the Revolution David supported Robespierre and the Jacobins. And for the next five years he was not only *the* artist of the Revolution but a political figure as well. In 1791 he began a tremendously elaborate painting, *The Oath of the Tennis Court* (pages 52–53)—a commemoration of the occasion when the deputies of the Third Estate, on June 20, 1789, swore not to disband until they had given France a constitution. His intention was to include portraits of every one of the deputies, but since too many of the personages involved had become suspect, the picture never got beyond the state of a sketch and a mass of preliminary drawings.

During this time David rode very high. In 1792 he was elected a deputy in the convention and a member of the art commission, which made him the virtual art dictator of France. The commission made drastic reforms. Having earlier organized a petition among a group of artists, David now succeeded in abolishing the Academy (with its hated name, Académie Royale), along with all the secondary organizations that had trained craftsmen throughout the provinces. Whatever else the Academy had done, it had always preserved the technical traditions inherited from the old masters, and this mass abolition was a blow that affected French art from that time on.

But Frenchmen could hardly conceive of art without government sponsorship, and the Academy was replaced by a "Commune of the Arts," a body of three hundred members. Private patronage was supposed to vanish (one thinks of the Russian reforms), to be replaced by the Commune. The function of art would be to glorify the new ideals of the state and to record its triumphs (again, Russia today), and the state would purchase these patriotic pictures from open competitions.

The Commune of the Arts reigned for not quite two months. It took only that long for it to fall under the same accusations of favoritism and dictatorship that had been leveled against the Academy. It was replaced by a smaller replica of itself called the Popular and Republican Society of the Arts—also dominated by David. (Eventually—in 1795—this gave way to the Letters and Fine Arts division of the Institute of France, which became simply the old Royal Academy with a new name.)

Under David the government founded a National Museum of the Arts, the genesis of the Louvre, to inventory and preserve confiscated works of art from churches, the royal palaces, and the houses of émigrés. (It was to this

museum that David appointed his old benefactor Fragonard as a curator.) The government also set aside money to purchase works of art at private sales in order to keep them in the country, and David saved many pictures in this way, including some by Rubens and Rembrandt.

He was a busy man. In addition to these administrative functions he was in charge of commemorative monuments as well as popular celebrations and state funerals, which could be elaborate affairs involving, according to some of David's plans, virtually the entire population of Paris. And meanwhile he was still the state painter. There were plenty of martyrs and something had to be done about them. David's possible masterpiece, *Marat Assassinated* (see page 59), commemorated that colleague's murder in 1793 by Charlotte Corday.

During all this time the atmosphere was becoming more and more hysterical, and when David is judged, this hysteria must be remembered. He made no effort to save certain of his friends from the guillotine, but the reason could have been that he was convinced that they deserved it, not that he was afraid to risk his own neck. His ruthless treatment of the Academy, which after all had treated him well for more years than it had, in his opinion, treated him badly, can be easily explained as a personal vendetta. But it may also have been the result of his conviction that its system was inhibiting to art, especially an art that he sincerely believed must serve new purposes. But it is difficult to forgive him (and his colleagues) for the execution of the ineffectual young king who had been

his patron. David voted for the death of Louis XVI, and it was on this occasion that his wife left him.

Two years later, in 1794, David's triumphant progress suffered an interruption that threatened to be permanent. His friend Robespierre fell from power and went to the scaffold where he had sent so many others. David said that if necessary he would share a cup of hemlock with Robespierre, a form of classical suicide that he had celebrated in his painting *The Death of Socrates*, but the guillotine was another matter. David came to trial and is reported to have conducted himself badly on the stand, mumbling and sweating in his defense. But neither the mumble nor the sweat can really be held against a man whose speech was impaired and whose life was in danger.

David was imprisoned for four months, released, and then in 1795 rearrested and imprisoned for another two months. The Luxembourg Palace had been turned into a temporary prison for political offenders, and here, during his first incarceration, with a pleasant view of the gardens that he recorded in his only landscape (above), David spent his time planning a new picture as the start of a new career. His friends supplied him with materials for his work, and his wife forgave him. From his window he could see her or a nursemaid with his children, playing in the park.

The new picture was *The Sabines*, too often referred to with careless inaccuracy as *The Rape of the Sabines*. David chose not the episode of the Sabine women's abduction by the Romans but the subsequent one, when, having been taken to wife and begun families with their captors, the Sabine women intervened between their Roman husbands and their brothers and fathers who had come to rescue them. The Sabine woman Hersilie is shown at the center of a huge canvas with one arm stretched out in appeal toward the Roman Romulus and the other toward the Sabine Tatius—who pause at the moment of conflict—while other figures are disposed around them in an exceptionally orderly delineation of climactic confusion.

The Revolution having failed of the nobility of the Roman republic, David now made every effort to minimize the importance of his Revolutionary paintings and decided to devote himself to pure art. But his painting was again interpreted as a political allegory. *The Sabines* became a symbol of the new conciliatory mood in France, an appeal to the warring factions to pull themselves away from one another's throats for the good of the nation. David exhibited the picture for a fee, publishing a long defense of this unconventional practice (which in the old days would have resulted in his expulsion from the Academy) and defending, also, the nudity of his warriors, which he imagined to be in the Greek tradition. Greek glory and grace, as they were then envisioned, now preoccupied him at the cost of Roman grandeur, and although *The Sabines* is a chilly picture, it seems a decidedly sensuous one in comparison with *The Oath of the Horatii.*

The admission fees brought David a small fortune, with which he bought a farm-estate, but *The Sabines* did more than secure him a fortune and a new place in popular favor. Napoleon was much impressed by it. His private taste in art ran to a more sentimental style, preferably with lascivious overtones, but he recognized in David the perfect artist as propagandist for the image he was developing of himself as a counterpart of the Roman emperors of conquest. He never gave David the dictatorial powers he had had during the Revolution, but he showered him with honors and David became again, in effect, the head of a school of official art.

Although his painting had become more graceful, with an increased concern for such gentle subjects as love, David was still interested in the re-creation of the ancient world as he imagined it. His influence on fashion and decoration can hardly be overestimated. The Directoire and Empire styles are virtually his invention. Women imitated the gauzy costume of Hersilie in *The Sabines,* even to the extent of exposing their breasts. The pieces of furniture he had had constructed from his designs, for use in his pictures and incidental use in his studio, became the models for the decoration of fashionable rooms everywhere.

By the time Napoleon declared himself emperor in 1804, David was fifty-six years old and quite content with

Marat Assassinated (1793) has become, in the words of one art historian, "the Pietà of the Revolution." The dead Republican leader, murdered in his bathtub by a young gentlewoman named Charlotte Corday, is shown holding a letter from her in one hand and in the other, the quill pen that had been busy sentencing his political enemies to death.

his renunciation of politics. He was indefatigably industrious as a portrait painter, and in his execution of the paintings Napoleon commissioned, he employed enough assistants to amount to a school. Between 1805 and 1807 he painted the largest of his Napoleonic tributes, a mass group-portrait, thirty feet long and twenty feet high, of the Coronation, in which Napoleon, already crowned, places a second wreath on the head of Josephine. The painting is an efficiently executed bore that may be found in any French history textbook or that may be seen in the Louvre, where it is surrounded by crowds every Sunday.

When Napoleon fell and the Bourbons were restored, David sent all his compromising pictures to his house in the country and was left as undisturbed as if he had never been a right-hand man of the emperor. But when Napoleon re-entered Paris for his ephemeral reign of the Hundred Days, he saw David; and in an incautious moment the painter signed the *Acte additional.* As a result of this pledge of loyalty he was exiled in 1816, and spent the remaining nine years of his life in Brussels, where he died in 1825 at the age of seventy-seven. He was a contented old man during these last years, and though barred from returning to Paris, he was still highly regarded there, receiving pilgrimage visits from his admirers. He continued to paint to the end—usually in a rather desiccated way—and concluded his career with a canvas called *Mars Disarmed by Venus and the Graces.* It shows an incredibly, almost mawkishly handsome nude Mars disposed upon a draped couch against the background of a classical frieze; except for clouds beneath his feet that identify the scene as Olympus, he might be in the house of the most beautiful of all Greek courtesans, the Venus who seductively leans toward him with one hand on his thigh.

In the tradition by which David's other paintings were given political interpretations, this one could be interpreted as his final conclusion that war and violence—in the person of Mars—must inevitably yield to the charms of love and the arts. And one must admit that David's life, if hardly a typical one, was at least a unique proof of that premise.

This eleventh in a series by John Canaday, art critic of The New York Times, *is adapted from his forthcoming book* Lives of the Painters (*W. W. Norton & Co., Inc.*)

MAX LOREAU

Jean Dubuffet, the contemporary French master, has just completed his twenty-third period—which he devoted to the making of jigsaw patterns

ALL PAINTINGS FROM "JEAN DUBUFFET, 1962–66," EXHIBITED AT THE SOLOMON R. GUGGENHEIM MUSEUM, N.Y.

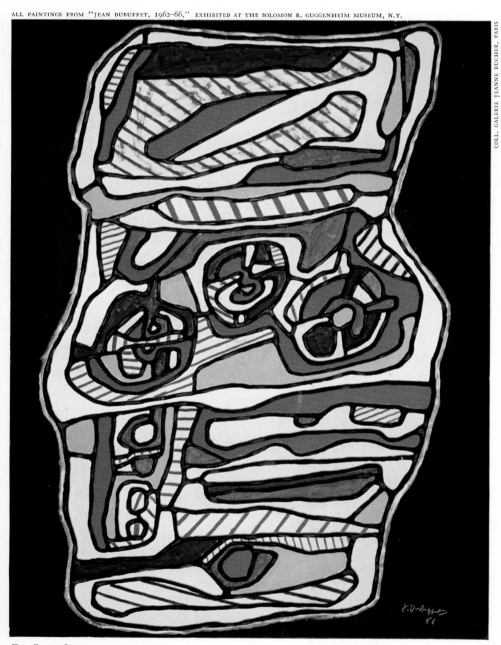

COLL. GALERIE JEANNE BUCHER, PARIS

GAS STOVE I, VINYL, 1966

Jean Dubuffet may well be the most restlessly prolific artist of this decade. The paintings shown here represent his latest work and, by his own reckoning, his twenty-third period.

Dubuffet rocketed to fame after 1944 and sustained his reputation through the fifties by producing "primitive" works based on his theory of *l'art brut* (art brutal, savage, and vulgar), reminiscent of the theatre of Alfred Jarry and Antonin Artaud.

His latest period was initiated in 1963 when he published the booklet *l'Hourloupe* (a meaningless word invented by Dubuffet), containing drawings made with red and blue ball point pens. His intent was, and is, to rearrange cityscapes, people, and the most familiar of everyday objects into jigsaw-puzzle patterns, to teach the eye to look at things afresh.

In keeping with the current fashion, art critics have doggedly searched Dubuffet's water taps and stoves and scissors for evidence of alienation—and found it. They are, after all, "fragmented"; they are labyrinths.

Yet, like children's puzzles, they are also fun. They are even—as one critic has pointed out—"anthropomorphic." That is, they imply the people who use the objects. Some of them have human forms. Dubuffet, in his twenty-third period, has come some distance from the art of assault and cruelty.

COFFEE POT III, VINYL ON PAPER, 1965

REASONABLE FIGURE OF SCISSORS, VINYL, 1966

PIANO, VINYL, 1966

TYPEWRITER III, INK, 1964

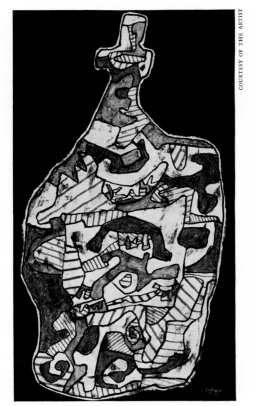

BOTTLE III, VINYL ON PAPER, 1965

WHEELBARROW VI, INK, 1964

LADDER IV, INK, 1966

AMPLIFICATION OF A TAP, VINYL, 1965

PERPETUATION OF THE HOUR, VINYL, 1965

ADELMANN

Günter Haese began by taking apart
a watch—and ended up with
these elegant little sculptural fancies

SCULPTURES FROM MARLBOROUGH FINE ART LTD., LONDON, EXCEPT WHERE OTHERWISE NOTED

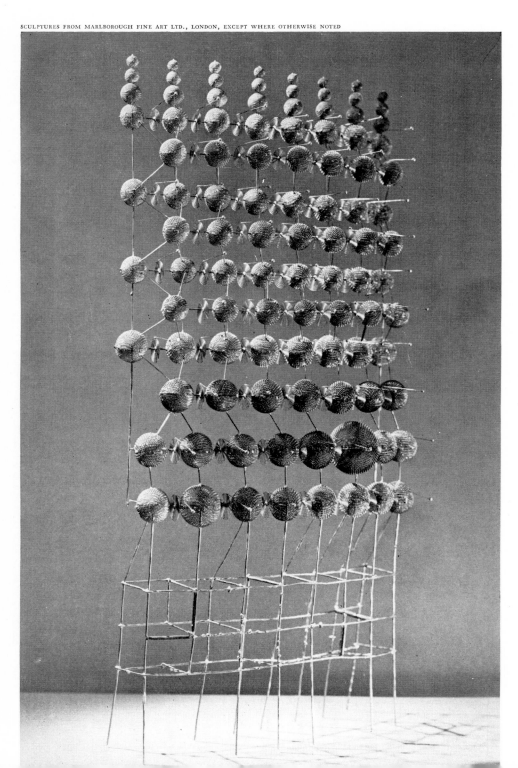

HOUSE OF LORDS, 1963

Born in 1924 and reared in Germany, Günter Haese had a singularly undistinguished career as a young artist. He studied for some time at the Düsseldorf Academy and with the German sculptor Ewald Mataré, and, beginning in 1959, he earned his living executing reliefs and mosaics for new buildings in Düsseldorf.

Then, in 1961, he happened to dismantle a clock and became fascinated —like any boy—with its tiny gears, balance wheels, spindles, and tension springs. He first arranged the parts in rather dull fashion, contenting himself with reproducing their shadows two-dimensionally on paper. But by the following year he was constructing elegant little sculptures made of brass and copper such as the ones seen here, that need only the slightest breath of air to set them trembling.

Critics have described his work as having wit, grace, and sophistication (and they have pointed out, too, that Paul Klee's fanciful imagery has influenced Haese), and those qualities are quite apparent in his "A New Moon," "New York Spring," "Rare Cactus," and "Flirt." There is a stateliness, as well, in his whimsical "House of Lords," and even a tenderness in "After the Rain." They are qualities all the more astonishing and welcome when one thinks that they were, in motivation and material, products of the modern technological age.

AFTER THE RAIN, 1965

RARE CACTUS, 1963

A NEW MOON, 1963

NEW YORK SPRING, 1965

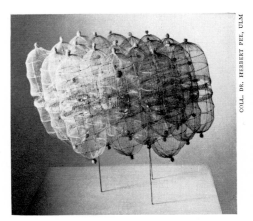

OASIS, 1964

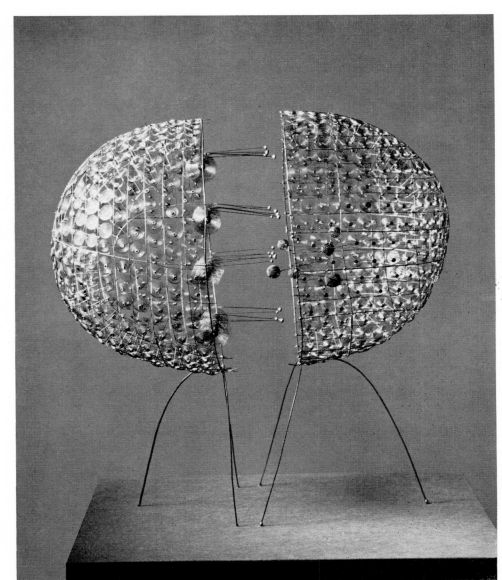

FLIRT, 1965

63

Forbidden by Hitler to paint, Emil Nolde secretly turned out water colors; of all his work, these, his "unpainted pictures," are among his greatest

A GROUP OF CHILDREN

Emil Nolde, who was born one hundred years ago and died in 1956, was an anti-Semite and a German jingoist. By an ironic turn of history, he got what he deserved in 1937: Hitler declared his art "degenerate," confiscated 1,052 of his works, and in 1941 informed Nolde that he was altogether forbidden to paint.

But if Nolde's moral sensibilities were degenerate, his paintings were not, as these diminutive water colors from the current show organized by M. Knoedler & Co. illustrate. Nolde called them his "unpainted pictures" —for they were intended as studies for oils. He painted in water color during the war because he feared oils would betray him if Gestapo members should come to his house, in North Schleswig, and smell the paint. He had been a painter of landscapes and religious subjects and a pioneer expressionist, but during the war he turned mainly to vignettes of lonely old men and women and frightened, huddling children.

Nolde achieved his luminous, haunting colors by allowing wet paint to flow over wet paper, and then later drawing the outlines. If the subjects are occasionally reminiscent of Edvard Munch's fantasies, the bold command of water color was unprecedented—and it appears likely that Nolde will be remembered more for his water colors than for his oils.

ANCIENT COUPLE

THREE VETERANS

BY THE SEA

THREE HEADS

LONESOME COUPLE

IN THE THEATRE

TWO LADY-FRIENDS

DANCING WOMEN

65

QUEEN CHRISTINA

A woman who wished she were a man;
a queen who aspired to be a scholar;
a Protestant who turned to Rome;
a monarch who loved power but gave up her crown—
such were the paradoxes of Christina of Sweden

Queen Christina of Sweden was one of those people who seem born to hit the headlines. The daughter and only child of Gustavus Adolphus, the most famous prince of his age; queen of Sweden at the age of six, when her father was killed in 1632 on a German battlefield in the Thirty Years' War; the idol of European intellectuals while still little more than a girl; the despair of her councilors and country on account of her resolute refusal to marry; a source of universal astonishment for her dramatic renunciation of her throne at the age of twenty-seven; the toast of Catholic Europe when, to the horror of her fellow Protestants, she announced her conversion to Rome; volatile, capricious, extravagant, her habits and manners eccentric, her sexual inclinations bizarre. No doubt all royal personages in the seventeenth century lived their lives in a blaze of publicity, but somehow Christina contrived to obtain more than her fair share. If, at the end, she suffered the usual consequences of over-exposure, and died half-forgotten by the world, she had sufficiently impressed contemporaries with the brilliance and strangeness of her personality to remain a source of puzzlement to later generations.

The determination to impress and to puzzle was, of course, a deliberate part of the act. "One should aspire to be not a copy but an original," she once wrote, and no one could deny that she had done everything pos-

Seated on a rearing horse in this portrait by the French artist Sébastien Bourdon, Queen Christina of Sweden looks almost as boyish at twenty-six as her elegant young falconer.

sible to live up to her own maxim. Everything about her, starting with her appearance, belied the ordinary and the expected. The court painters naturally did their best to make their royal sitter's portrait conform to the conventional canons of taste, but the sallow face, the strong, hooked nose, the protruding, slightly myopic eyes, and the unkempt, loosely hanging hair—all these features, like the queen's entire character, somehow refused to conform.

No queen was less queenly, in the conventional sense of the word, nor any woman less womanly. On this, all observers were agreed: "Despite her sex there is nothing feminine about her. Her voice is that of a man and likewise her manner of speech, her movements and gestures. . . . although she rides sidesaddle, she sways and bends her body in such a way that, unless one sees her from close quarters, it is easy to take her for a man. When she goes riding she wears a hat and waistcoat in the Spanish style. Only her skirt betrays her womanhood. . . . She seldom wears ornaments of gold and silver. Her hair she combs only once a week, at times no more than once a fortnight. On Sundays she takes half an hour to dress, on weekdays a quarter of an hour only. Sometimes, in the course of conversation, I have noticed that her clothes have been flecked with ink because she writes so much. Sometimes I have even noticed them to be ragged." ". . . very lively in her movements, actions and speech; without royal reserve in her unaffected behavior and extremely friendly to each and everyone in her manner, discourse and return of greetings; and on the whole intended by nature as a man, but become a woman, displaying qualities from both sexes in her vitality, aspirations and mode of living . . ."

As she grew older, these unusual characteristics became still more marked. Even the Grande Mademoiselle, the cousin of Louis XIV, herself one of the most formidable of all seventeenth-century royal ladies, was somewhat taken aback when she met Christina on her visit to France in 1656. "She is," decided Mademoiselle, "quite extraordinary"—hardly an extravagant verdict after an evening at the theatre during which Christina had distinguished herself by punctuating the performance with troopers' oaths and deep sighs, lying back in her chair and flinging out her legs on one side and the other, and "taking up attitudes that I have never seen, save in Trivelin and Jodelet, two buffoons, one French and the other Italian"; and all this to an incessant accompaniment of questions and comments, for as the whole world knew, Christina could rarely stop talking.

Hardly, one would have thought, the most prepossessing of characters. Yet the fact remains that she impressed, dazzled, and exercised an apparently irresistible attraction over some of the best minds in seventeenth-century Europe. When she was only seven, the lord high chancellor wrote to his brother: "Our young Queen is possessed of an extraordinary political genius." Her tutor, the liberal-minded Johannes Matthiae, found her a brilliantly apt pupil, with an insatiable thirst for knowledge. By the time she came of age in 1644, she knew most of the leading European languages; she spoke Latin as if it were her native tongue; she had a smattering of Greek, Hebrew, and Arabic; and she had read widely in philosophy, theology, mathematics, and astronomy. "Her

This gold-embroidered saddle was made in Paris for Christina's coronation. Originally a sidesaddle, it was later converted for the crowning of her successor, Charles Gustavus.

Majesty," said Axel Oxenstierna, the great Swedish statesman, "is a credit to her sex and age; God knows, how it rejoices me to see that she is not womanly, but of good heart and deep understanding."

"She is not womanly . . ." To Christina, as to most of her contemporaries, few words could have been more gratifying. To be born a woman was, in seventeenth-century eyes, to be born at a disadvantage; but to be born a woman on the throne was a disaster. Only rarely had some great queen, like Elizabeth I of England, managed to prevail over the fatal disabilities of her sex. When times were insecure—and *all* times were insecure in the Europe of the sixteenth and seventeenth centuries—the firm hand of a man at the tiller was regarded as essential, if the ship were not to run aground or founder on the rocks of rebellion. To no country did this rule of state apply more forcefully than to Sweden. A remote and barbaric outpost of Europe during the sixteenth century, it had suddenly, in the early seventeenth century, become a great Continental power. This had been achieved in a few short years by the military genius of Christina's father, Gustavus Adolphus, by the courage and disciplined organization of his armies, and by the skillful exploitation of a European demand for two of Sweden's few exportable commodities, copper and iron.

By 1632 the king of Sweden had become the arbiter of Europe's fortunes, and a new "Gothic" hegemony seemed about to be established over the Continent. But then, at the moment of triumph, disaster had struck with the death of Gustavus Adolphus at Lützen. The future of Sweden suddenly depended on the loyalty and responsibility of a handful of aristocratic councilors, and on the survival of a six-year-old girl.

It was not surprising that Christina was brought up to be a king; not surprising that, having been born the wrong sex—to the acute disappointment of her parents and her subjects—she should have done everything within her power to remedy an irremediable mistake; not surprising that she should have scorned the companionship of women, especially after watching the behavior of her neurotically unstable mother. By circumstance, by upbringing, by inclination, Christina was drawn to play the part of the man. She would turn for her models, not to the great women, but to the great men of past ages and, above all, to Alexander the Great. She would show her subjects, and the world, the mettle of which she was made. She would prove herself immune to that most fatal of all flaws in the feminine sex—the compliant dependence on men. In the prevailing fashion for Stoic philosophy she found an instrument ideally attuned to her needs, for Stoicism taught the art which of all arts she was most anxious to acquire, that of being totally self-sufficient in an envious, hostile, and egoistical world.

Christina spent the first twenty-seven years of her life in Stockholm Castle, seen here in a painting by Govaert Camphuysen. The queen's suite was in the cupolaed tower, right background; the building erected on piles over the moat (right) contained a lion presented to her on her coronation.

It was therefore with confidence, but also with a determination to listen and learn, that she threw herself into the tasks of government when she attained her majority at the age of eighteen. The 1640's were not an easy time in which to assume the royal power. All over Europe this was a decade of political and social upheaval, from which Sweden—weary of war, like most of the European powers—was unlikely to remain aloof. Throughout the queen's minority the regent Oxenstierna had lived in fear of a peasant rising, while the peasants themselves had watched with increasing alarm the growing power of an aristocracy no longer held in check by a forceful king. The tradition of hereditary monarchy had as yet struck no deep roots in Swedish soil, and Christina quickly became convinced that she was threatened by an aristocratic conspiracy to undermine and destroy the royal power and to establish a republican regime.

The principal objective of her policy was straightforward and simple: to recover the royal powers eroded during her own minority, and to ensure the hereditary succession of the Vasa line. Yet to carry this policy to a logical conclusion involved an action from which she instinctively shrank. She alone could perpetuate the direct succession, and yet she could not bring herself to contemplate the idea of marriage. Marriage, after all, required subordination, an end to self-sufficiency, and as the French ambassador reported home to Cardinal Mazarin, the queen "could never subordinate herself to a husband."

As for Christina, "I tell you here and now," she said to her Privy Council in 1649, "that it is impossible for me to marrry. So it must be, and I will not adduce reasons."

Once the decision was taken—and it seems already to have been taken by 1647, when she was only twenty-one—her policy was narrowed to the attainment of one overriding object: the solution of the succession problem without resort to matrimony. Her duty to her dynasty allowed of nothing less than that she solve the problem of the succession. Her duty to herself, as a unique being, allowed of nothing less than that she solve it without any permanent sacrifice of her own comfort and independence. She now brought to bear all her brilliant diplomatic skills to the unraveling of the complex knot which she had herself so assiduously tied. Her flat refusal ever to contemplate marriage inevitably precipitated a dynastic crisis, which was compounded in 1650 by growing social unrest and economic discontent. She now proceeded, with cynical skill, to play off the lower orders against the nobility and the nobility against the lower orders, and in the end emerged unscathed from the fray, bearing aloft the trophy she had sought: the recognition of Charles Gustavus (who had always stood in trembling awe of his alarming cousin) as hereditary heir to the Swedish crown.

No matter that for a few months the country had been shaken to its foundations, and had seemed on the brink of its own version of the English civil wars and the revolutionary movement in France known as the Fronde. As far as the queen was concerned, the risk had to be taken, and as it turned out, the gamble had triumphantly paid off. What, anyhow, was life without risk? There was in Christina's make-up a frenetic need for excitement. Later she was to write to Mazarin: "The news today threatens to engulf the world in a great tranquility; but I love the storm and fear the calm." Now, in the succession crisis, she had deliberately run the ship into the teeth of the storm, and had yet brought it triumphantly to port.

But Sweden was too small a stage for the type of role to which she aspired. Like her hero, Alexander, she needed new worlds to conquer. Denied by the misfortune of her sex the opportunity to win an empire by heroic feats of arms (her greatest desire, she later told the Grande Mademoiselle, was to take part in a battle), she chose instead to win it in a field ideally suited to her inclinations and abilities. Hers would be an empire over men's minds. The auguries at the beginning were not, it must be admitted, very promising. Those serried ranks of wooden-faced Swedish divines staring solemnly out of their portrait frames would hardly seem very congenial company for a queen who prided herself on her catholicity of outlook and her intellectual vivacity. The Renaissance had come late to Sweden; the country's climate was unpromising; its religion was dour. "Men's minds seem to freeze as the water freezes," remarked a shivering Descartes, who came to Stockholm in 1649 at the queen's invitation, and succumbed within a few months to the rigors of a Swedish winter.

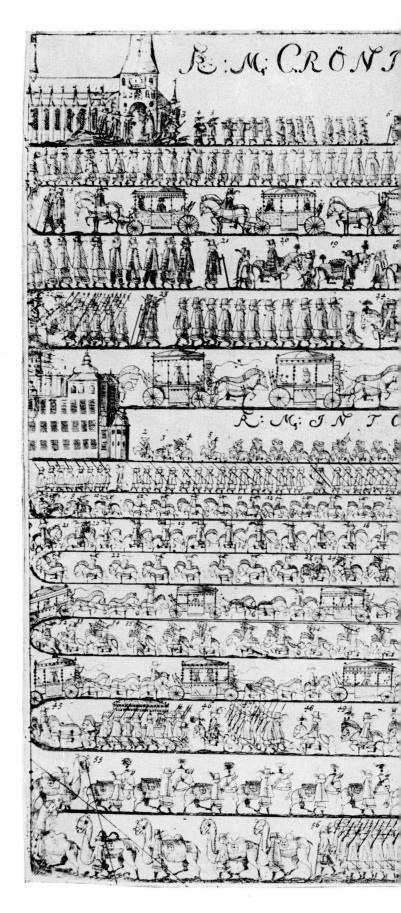

Yet it was in these unpromising surroundings that Christina set out to create for herself a court life which would dazzle and allure the best minds in Europe. In an age of patronage she would be the greatest patron of them all. In carrying out her design she enjoyed, and exploited to the full, certain important advantages. The victorious Swedish armies, campaigning in Central Europe, had sent back to Stockholm, at the queen's insistent request, a stream of valuable trophies—books and *objets d'art* and paintings, culminating in the greatest prize of all, the magnificent picture collection assembled at Prague at the end of the sixteenth century by Emperor Rudolph II. As the castle of the Three Crowns at Stockholm became filled with these precious articles, Christina required curators and librarians to study and classify them. Revolutions in England and France had eliminated—the first permanently, the second temporarily—two of her principal rivals in the international patronage stakes, Charles I and Cardinal Mazarin, part of whose library she managed to acquire. As surprising reports of the brilliance and erudition of the young Swedish queen percolated southward, scholars for the first time turned their gaze toward an almost unknown North.

Christina was quick to seize her chance. Distinguished

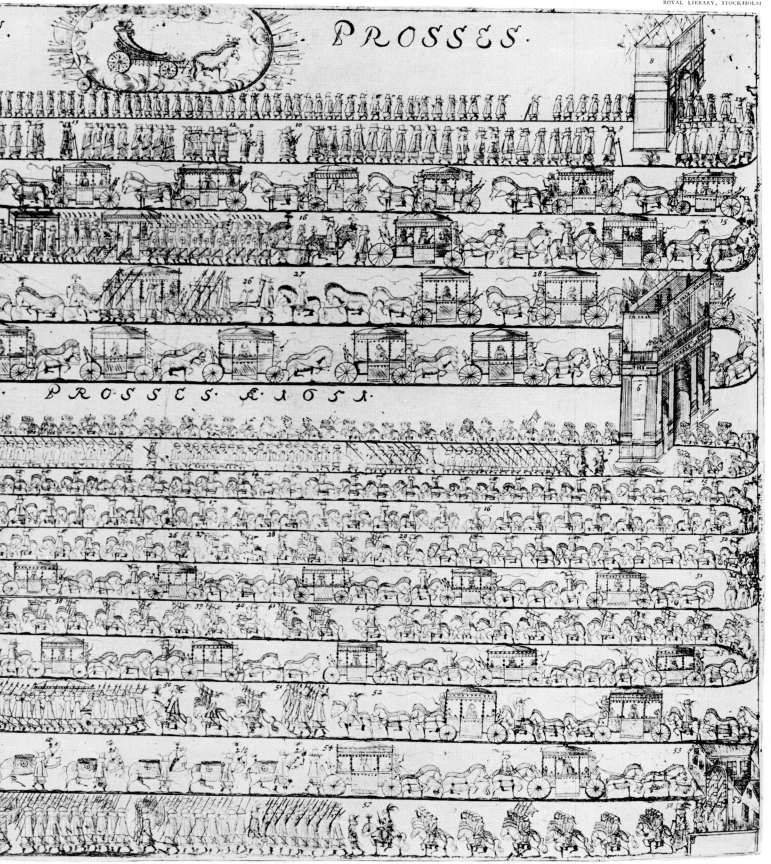

A Swedish artist depicted Christina's coronation procession (it took place in 1650, not 1651, as the drawing is inscribed), crowding the scene into a snake dance. The line winds upward through a triumphal arch to Stockholm Castle (middle left) and on to the church (upper left) where she was crowned. In a carriage, hovering above it all, is the queen.

In this imaginary scene painted about 1700, Christina is surrounded by luminaries of the Paris salons. She sits at a table, right, with Elizabeth of the Palatinate, listening to a discourse by René Descartes (opposite Christina). Actually, the philosopher died six years before the young Swedish queen's visit in 1656.

European men of letters, Isaac Vossius and Claudius Salmasius from Holland, and, above all, the great Descartes, received flattering invitations to assist, enlighten, and instruct the queen. She set up an academy, in the proper manner of her age. She patronized the arts and sciences, brought stage designers from Italy, and commissioned court ballets with novel choreography and scenic apparatus. She discussed difficult philological and philosophical problems with learned European correspondents and thrilled as some newly acquired Greek manuscript was laid before her at court. Her enthusiasm and erudition soon brought her the universal reputation to which she aspired. Pascal, who had never met her, in 1652 sent her his calculating machine, with an accompanying letter which eloquently testifies to Christina's fame among men of letters: "I know, my Lady, that I might well be judged presumptuous in offering this calculating machine to Your Majesty. I was moved thereto by the union in your person of two qualities both of which fill me with

wonder and reverence, namely absolute sovereignty and sound learning. . . . Mankind, being led by nature to desire that which is most complete, had till now hoped in vain for the spectacle of such a ruler above all others. All kings and all scholars were so created that they could only fulfill the half of that which was desired: the crowning glory was kept waiting for our lifetime. That degree of completeness, which men could not attain, has been realized through a young Queen, in whom the strength of experience is united with the tenderness of youth, the liberty of study with the burdens of kingship, the excellence of knowledge with the grace of womanly nature."

Even allowing for the obligatory panegyrics, this was handsome praise, especially from so fastidious a scholar as Pascal. Perhaps if he had met her, his raptures would have been more moderately phrased. It was true that men of letters, at their first meeting, were captivated by her gaiety, the quickness of her wit, and the liveliness of what the English ambassador, that cultivated Puritan, Bulstrode Whitelocke, called her "pleasant intermixed discourses." But by the second or third meeting, it became apparent that the discourses were a good deal too intermixed. Christina's quick mind would dart here and there, picking up and dropping again some point which momentarily engaged her attention, but which she never had the patience to examine and probe. At heart, the scholar-queen remained a dilettante.

Nor was Pascal entirely correct in his assumption that Christina had achieved a perfect union of "the liberty of study with the burdens of kingship." The liberty seemed increasingly restricted, the burdens increasingly intolerable. Christina was always a woman at war both with herself and her surroundings. The brilliance and sophistication of her court seemed ill-attuned to the more prosaic background of contemporary Swedish life. The free-ranging philosophical discussions jarred with the stiff, dogmatic Lutheranism which the daughter of Gustavus Adolphus and the queen of Protestant Sweden was expected to uphold. Some of her most stimulating intellectual companions and correspondents were members of the Roman Church, and she gradually became convinced that she would find in Catholicism that intellectual freedom which her own brand of Protestantism seemed to deny her.

A woman who aspired to be a man; a queen who aspired to be a scholar; a Protestant who had begun to turn longingly toward Rome. The paradoxes multiplied, setting up internal strains and stresses which were increasingly difficult to contain. But she must at all costs remain the master of her fate, in accordance with the teachings of the Stoic philosophers whose disciple she had become. The inner defeat must be presented, both to the world and to herself, as a victory. It must appear not as an act of surrender but as a triumphant assertion of the will. "I have it in my thoughts and resolution," she confided to the astonished English ambassador, "to quit the crown of Sweden and to retire myself unto a private life, as much more suitable to my contentment, than the great cares and troubles attending upon the government of my kingdom; and what think you of this resolution?"

Abdications were rare in European history. The only recent example was that of the emperor Charles V, care-worn and weary when he handed over the government of Germany and Spain to his brother and son. The abdication of a young and successful queen, in the prime of life, would therefore appear an act of startling novelty, the dramatic assertion of a will which had retained its independence to the last. With characteristic energy and determination Christina set out to win her way. Having saved the principle of hereditary monarchy, she felt free to ignore the protests of her councilors and the pleas of

Christina entered Rome with typical flourish: she waited outside the city until the College of Cardinals, at her bidding, came forward to escort her.

her subjects. She had done her duty by her dynasty and her people. Why should she not now be allowed to lead her own life as she wished, surrounded by beautiful objects and entertained by the company of scholars and savants, far away from the cares and boredom of Swedish public life?

Her determination to join the Church of Rome was as yet known only to the two Jesuits whom she had secretly summoned to Sweden to answer her innumerable questions about the tenets of their faith. Her destination once she had renounced the crown was still uncertain, even to herself. She toyed with the idea of removing to Spa, or even of remaining on Swedish soil. It was some time before she hit on the ideal place for her retreat— Rome, the capital of the arts, the center of her new-found faith, the only city in which she, a queen, would have no need to acknowledge the sovereignty of any temporal power.

In 1653, in great secrecy, she began preparations for her residence abroad. The palace apartments were quietly emptied, the precious books and manuscripts packed into crates, the most beautiful (although not the most religiously edifying) tapestries taken down, the best pictures singled out for removal. The gallery in the palace at Stockholm contained more than eight hundred paintings, but Christina arranged for only some eighty of these to be shipped abroad. The palace collection was a better memorial to the tastes of Rudolph II, from whom so much of it came, than to those of Christina, whose predilections are revealed by the choice she made of the pictures to accompany her into exile.

Her German and Flemish paintings were left behind without remorse. She had no use for the northern masters, as she explained in a letter to the Duke of Bracciano several years after the arrival of Rudolph's pictures in Stockholm: "There is an infinite range of items, but apart from some thirty or forty Italian originals, I discount them all. There are works by Albrecht Dürer and other German masters whose names I do not know but who would arouse the profound admiration of anyone apart from myself. But I do declare that I would exchange them all for two Raphaels, and I think that even this would be doing them too much honor." In accordance with these somewhat restricted canons of taste, she took with her the works of the masters she most admired—Titian, Veronese, Correggio—while sending one of the finest works in her collection, Dürer's *Adam and Eve*, to that other great royal collector, Philip IV of Spain.

While these treasures were being quietly shipped abroad, the queen was preparing for the most historic event of her life—the surrender of her crown. On June 6, 1654, in the great hall of Uppsala Castle, the crown was formally removed from Christina's head, and she was ceremonially divested of her royal robes. Then the regalia and the realm were transferred to the new king, Charles X Gustavus. Christina herself professed to be unconcerned. "I am not in the least anxious," she had written, "about the final applause. I know that the scene I have to perform is not composed according to the laws of the theatre. It is a lot to ask that what is strong, manly, and powerful should win acceptance. I know that few will judge to my advantage . . ." She would be as self-sufficient, as indifferent to praise or blame, in surrendering her crown as she had been self-sufficient in the wearing

of it, and she played the part to perfection.

But how long would the façade stand firm? The prolonged second half of Christina's life suggested that it was perhaps easier to be a queen regnant than a queen redundant. She set off on her self-imposed exile in great style, incognito, disguised as a nobleman, a gun on her shoulder and a sword at her side. She stopped briefly at Hamburg and then moved on to Antwerp, where she lived for four months in the richly appointed house of a Portuguese Jew, surrounded by the treasures she had brought from Stockholm. Then, in December, 1654, she entered Brussels in a golden barge, to the accompaniment of a grand municipal fireworks display. It was here in Brussels, on Christmas Eve, that she secretly abjured Lutheranism in the presence of the governor, the Archduke

Leopold William, afraid that a public pronouncement at this stage would jeopardize the financial arrangements she had made with her subjects before leaving Sweden.

From Brussels she moved south toward her final goal, Italy; but Pope Alexander VII decided that he could not receive her in the Papal States with the appropriate honors unless she had first publicly proclaimed her conversion to Rome. This she did at Innsbruck, on November 3, 1655. Transformed into the heroine of Catholic Europe, she crossed into Italy with a retinue two hundred and fifty strong and was feted by one town after another on her royal progress south. On December 23, 1655, she rode into Rome, escorted by most of the College of Cardinals, themselves on horseback too. Slowly the procession moved through the gaily decorated streets to the richly adorned basilica of St. Peter's, and from there the queen was conducted to the papal apartments. Here she did her obeisance, the obligatory three genuflections, to a deeply moved pope. No pontificate could have wished a more glorious achievement than the spectacular conversion of the daughter of the Protestant hero Gustavus Adolphus.

Rome, as Christina saw it on her arrival, was a city in the process of being transformed by the genius of Bernini. Everywhere, churches and palaces were being rebuilt, and handsome piazzas laid out, in all the monumental splendor of the now fashionable style of the baroque. One of the most impressive of all the city's palaces, the great Palazzo Farnese, was placed at Christina's disposal by its owner, the Duke of Parma, and it was here that she spent the first months of her residence in Rome. No setting could have been more appropriate for the illustrious new arrival. In its superb galleries she could display to perfection her magnificent paintings and sculptures; in its ornate salons she could receive and entertain the nobles, the cardinals, the diplomats, who vied to do her honor. She became for a season the queen of the baroque city, the center of attraction at theatres, the guest of honor at lavish banquets given by cardinals who compromised between the demands of this world and those of the next by offering at their tables exquisite representations of the Passion, modeled entirely in sugar.

Unfortunately, Christina soon showed that she was not quite that earnest daughter of the church envisaged by the pope when he first welcomed her at the Vatican. Her strange habits and outspoken tongue scandalized a Rome

TEXT CONTINUED ON PAGE 78

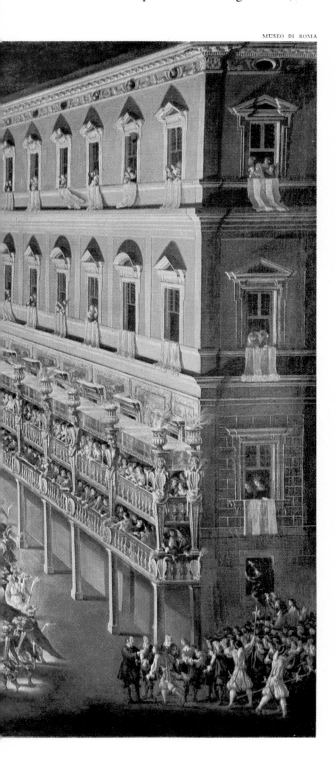

An evening carrousel is performed in Christina's honor at the Palazzo Barberini in Rome (she watched from the lower box in the center of the palace façade). The pageant, which took place in February, 1656, featured a mock battle between teams of "Cavaliers" and "Amazons"—280 performers in all.

75

BORGHESE GALLERY, ROME—COURTESY *Life*

KAISER FRIEDRICH MUSEUM, BERLIN—BRUCKMANN GIRAUDON

Of the paintings she took with her to Rome, two she especially admired were these companion pieces by Correggio. Each represents one of Jupiter's many seductions of mortal women—Danae (above), in which he appears as a cloudburst of gold, and Leda and the Swan (left). The sensuality of these paintings proved a bit too much for one of their later owners, Louis d'Orleans, who in a fit of temper gouged out Leda's head from the canvas. But soon afterward a contemporary artist gave her a new one that, with a few later restorations, has survived to the present day.

From a Perugian nunnery Christina bought five altarpiece panels by Raphael, who was her favorite artist. Above is The Procession to Calvary

Among Christina's 2,000 objets d'art was this ebony and silver clock of Venus on a chariot.

In Giuseppe Arcimboldo's The Gardener *a fantasy of fruits and flowers is transformed into a human being.*

Mars and Venus United by Love *was one of ten Veroneses Christina's armies sent from Prague. It is now in New York.*

Christina believed that this Greek head of about 300 B.C. was a portrait of her hero, Alexander the Great.

*While other guests stand around hungry, Christina dines sumptuously with
Pope Clement IX under his canopy. But she had to sit at a lower table.*

TEXT CONTINUED FROM PAGE 75

that, for all its ostentation and splendor, proved in some respects to be as strait-laced as Stockholm. The Roman Church was not, after all, that haven of free thought which Christina had fondly imagined it to be. She visited monasteries and churches, she surrounded herself with artists and scholars, but somehow the old restlessness refused to disappear. There were constant financial worries, for the pension she was receiving from Sweden was irregularly paid. Above all, she found that she could not bear her new isolation from the realm of public affairs. She began to toy again with thoughts of a crown—Naples, possibly, or Poland, or perhaps even Sweden—and in 1656 she suddenly surprised Rome by announcing that she was leaving Italy for a season.

Nominally the queen's journey was designed to make possible a meeting with Charles X of Sweden, with whom she hoped to settle her financial affairs, but it was also intended as an occasion to explore with Cardinal Mazarin the possibility of securing French help to make her queen of Naples. The visit to France, however, ended in disaster. Discussions with Mazarin continued over a long period and seemed to be reaching a satisfactory conclusion. But then, somehow, the secret details of the plan to place her on the Neapolitan throne leaked out to the world. Christina had been betrayed, and the suspect was her own master of the horse, the Neapolitan Marquis Monaldesco.

On November 10, 1657, she summoned Monaldesco to her presence in the Galerie des Cerfs at the French royal castle of Fontainebleau, where she was at that time residing, and had him interrogated for two hours. Monaldesco confessed to the charges and threw himself at the queen's feet, begging for mercy; but Christina was unmoved.

Then and there she sentenced him to death, and when the priest who was in attendance followed her out of the room to remonstrate at this somewhat unusual behavior in a royal castle on foreign soil, she replied that "she owned the right of a ruler to execute justice among her subjects at all times and in all places; she was answerable for her actions before God and none other." Treason was unforgivable, mercy unthinkable. Back in the Galerie des Cerfs, three armed men cut down the wretched Monaldesco, but the heavy mail shirt under his clothes prevented their swords from striking home, and it took a quarter of an hour or more to complete the bloody business.

The barbarous slaughter of Monaldesco may have seemed to Christina no more than an act of common justice, but to most of Europe it appeared in a very different light. Here was a piece of extravagant revenge for unknown, and undoubtedly sinister, motives. From this moment, the queen's political credit was totally destroyed;

*This punctured mail shirt and sword, in a museum at Fontainebleau,
are thought to have been worn by Monaldesco at his execution.*

Christina's friend Pope Alexander VII, and her confidant Cardinal Azzolino, right, were both portrayed by the sculptor Bernini.

there was no chance now of a comeback on the European stage. A private life was all that remained open to her, and she duly returned to Rome. Here, in 1659, she acquired the palace which was to be her home for the remaining thirty years of her life. This was the Palazzo Riario, a fine Renaissance building with superb gardens, on the Vatican side of the Tiber. She furnished the palace with great splendor and filled it with her collections, which she was continually enlarging. She fitted out an observatory, dabbled in alchemy and scientific experiments, received an endless stream of scholars and connoisseurs, founded an academy, and entertained her guests at brilliant spectacles and at concerts and operas with specially commissioned music by Scarlatti.

Yet there was still something missing. Reduced to her own resources, she found that she was not quite as self-sufficient as she had formerly believed; and then, suddenly and humiliatingly, she fell in love with an elegant member of the College of Cardinals, Decio Azzolino. Her tastes in the past had run as much to women as to men, but always she had prided herself on her ability to dominate the passions which affected lesser mortals. This time, self-command was both more necessary and less easy than before. The cardinal, who had long been her confidant and adviser, did nothing to show that her extravagant letters met with any response on his own part, and for once Christina realized that she had been thwarted and defeated.

Was it wounded pride and a sense of humiliation that now made her abandon the philosophy that had guided her conduct for so much of her life? "Stoicism," she wrote, "was my philosophy for a long time past, but it did not bring me happiness." In her disillusionment she turned to its opposite extreme, the newly fashionable quietism of the Spanish priest Miguel de Molinos. Not activity, but resignation and surrender, became the order of the day; and, for a time, she seems to have found a certain peace in this gently mystical movement.

It was a strange transformation for a woman who had always believed that the exercise of the "manly" virtues would enable her to control and shape her fate. But her reactions had always been original—or had they, after all? For the intellectual world, which she had so consistently admired, had also turned its back on the stoicism of the mid-seventeenth century. The queen who had always aspired to be "not a copy but an original" had in reality conformed more closely to the successive modes and fashions of her century than she realized. One of the many paradoxes of Christina's life was that the "century of Queen Christina" was the century of a sprightly, shallow, slightly pathetic woman, deliberately insensitive to the world around her, and yet at heart too sensitive to the currents of her age.

As the years passed, it became clear that there was something about Christina which neither time nor fashion could subdue. Old at sixty-two, and very ill, she had little time to live. But, furious at finding that she had been deceived by a servant, she rose up from her chair on April 14, 1689, in a desperate attempt to seize him. The effort proved too much for her, and she collapsed unconscious on the floor. Five days later she was dead. It was a fittingly grotesque conclusion to a tempestuous life. Indomitable, defiant, Christina after all remained unique to the end.

J. H. Elliott is a fellow of Trinity College, Cambridge, and lecturer in history. His article on Cortes and Montezuma appeared in the November, 1963, issue of HORIZON.

THE GUITAR

After a century of velvet sounds, in which the blended timbres of the symphony orchestra held sway, the musical world is now in the grip of a great resurgence of pure twang. From Nashville and Liverpool, or Bombay and Yokohama, come the incessant jangling and thrumming of plucked instruments that have suddenly become dear to our ears: the baroque harpsichord, whose effervescent ping is threatening to displace the felt-struck thud of the piano; the Renaissance lute, undergoing a second golden age launched by Julian Bream; the banjo, up from slavery and now indispensable to any movie sound track that aspires to Americana; the seven-hundred-year-old Indian sitar, which sounds like a hail of broken icicles when Ravi Shankar runs his plectrum across its strings; its cousin the South Indian vina, which twangs for agonizing moments of indecision before finally settling down to a definite note; the six-foot Japanese koto, thirteen strings, all body and no neck; the heike-biwa, the sarod, the samisen, the p'i-p'a, yueh-chin, chirar, rebab, santir, ombi, vambi, nanga.

But above all it is the guitar that currently finds work for idle hands: at last

Three guitars from three countries and three centuries are shown opposite: a Venetian model of the late 1500's (left); an ivory and ebony Spanish guitar of the next century (below); and a French guitar from 1749, encrusted with mother-of-pearl. The dwarf guitarist at right dates from 1622, and the photograph of Elvis Presley (above) is from 1956.

CHARLES TRAINOR—MIAMI *Daily News*

"The wine cups of daybreak
are shattered.
The Lament
of the guitar begins.
It is useless to silence it."

By FREDERIC V. GRUNFELD

guess there were eight or ten million guitars in circulation in the United States alone, and there is no foreseeable end to their proliferation. This staggering statistic must be interpreted to mean that all our major factions—college students, high-school dropouts, peace marchers, paratroopers in green berets, and Southern gubernatorial candidates—accept the guitar as a universal means of communication.

The signs of this sonic revolution are everywhere. In France recently I saw how the tradition-minded luthiers of the Vosges have shifted over to producing guitars instead of violins and cellos. The same thing is happening in Germany. In Russia—even in Siberia—the students are playing guitars rather than balalaikas. Andrés Segovia, the grand old man of guitarism, plays to packed houses wherever he appears: when I heard him at the London Festival Hall last June the huge auditorium was packed to the rafters, but you could have heard a pin drop.

In Britain there was a day of national mourning not too long ago when one of the army of young electric-guitar players was electrocuted as he went to plug in his amplifier—the first guitarist since Lully to die of service-connected causes. At about the same time the Danish foreign minister, on a visit to South America, seems to have made more friends and influenced more people than did de Gaulle on his trip to that continent, by the Machiavellian expedient of serenading his hosts on the guitar. Could *le grand Charles* have

81

hoped to do as much on the musette? Certainly the guitar has never had it so ubiquitous; not even in its Iberian heyday when, after a battle between Spaniards and Portuguese, the losing army took to the hills and left (it was said) 11,000 guitars upon the battlefield.

In the process of becoming universal the guitar has lost most of its former social connotations and extramusical overtones. To have played the instrument in 1550 would have identified you as a Spanish *gracioso*; perhaps as a Don Juan. If you were playing one in 1620 and were not Spanish, it would have stigmatized you as belonging among "the charlatans and saltimbanques who use it for strumming, to

Moorish troubador with cittern, 13th century

which they sing villanelles and other foolish *lumpen*-songs." Around 1820 a guitar would have marked you as a nature-loving romantic of Keatsian tendencies. As Shelley expresses it:

"The artist wrought this loved guitar,
  And taught it justly to reply,
To all who question skillfully,
  In language gentle as thine own;
Whispering in enamoured tone
Sweet oracles of woods and dells,
And summer winds in sylvan
    cells . . ."

During the 1930's, on the other hand,

possession of a guitar was prima-facie evidence that you belonged to a Young Marxists' Chowder and Marching Society. Today, with the whole nation awash with the thrum and thrust of guitars, it means nothing more than that you are taking the shortest known route to what the Montgomery Ward Catalogue calls "the romance of traditional folk and country-western music as well as your own mode of self-expression in song" (at prices ranging from $16.50 to $219.95).

From a psychological standpoint, however, the guitar is still a very powerful symbol. The young man who brings a guitar to a party is serving notice, in effect, that he is a modern Leatherstocking type, sexually on the *qui vive*, a man who can "handle women." These, at any rate, are some of the associations that derive from the mystique of the foot-loose and fancy-free guitar—an image to which the serenader, the range rider, Huddy Ledbetter, and the French gypsy jazzman Django Reinhardt have all contributed their share.

Yet the deeper, subconscious significance of the twang is much older than that, and apparently lies buried in the earliest aural experiences of the human race. The original ancestor of all plucked instruments—indeed the earliest instrument of which we possess a definite record—is the hunting bow that does double duty as a musical bow, like the one shown in a cave drawing at Les Trois Frères, in France. The sorcerer-priest in that early Stone Age hunting scene has a musical bow fastened to the mouth of his mask; he holds it out with his left hand and twangs it with his right. This selfsame instrument—essentially a one-string guitar using the mouth as a resonating cavity and the skull as a sounding board—still does yeoman service as the okongo in certain parts of Africa, and produces some of the most glorious *boinging* and *dwoinging* sounds known to mankind.

It has not escaped the mythologists

that Apollo the god of archers is also Apollo the god of music, a circumstance that might reasonably be explained by the dualism of the bow. Apollo's lyre, at any rate, derives from this musical principle, and so do scores of other adaptations found the world over: fiber chords strung over turtle shells; wires mounted over clay pots; silken strings over calabash forms; gut strings stretched over wooden bowls in the shape of figs, or eggs, or muskmelons. But the history of what we call the guitar (as distinct from the other members of this numerous family of chordophones) begins at the point where the form of the instrument takes on the shape of a woman's body: softly rounded at the shoulders, curving inward at the waist, and concluding with another gently rounded curve at the bottom.

Some obviously soulless organographers have described the guitar as having a figure-eight shape, whereas in actual fact its outline is simply the classic admiring gesture of man delineating the form of woman. Poets always speak of her in these terms; in languages which assign genders to such things, the guitar is invariably feminine. *La mujer y la guitarra, para usarlas hay que templarlas* says an old Spanish proverb: to use a woman or a guitar one must know how to tune them or, literally, how to put them into a proper temper.

All of which may help to account for the upsurge of guitarism in this age of the unfettered libido. A motivational researcher might find that its popularity is based on its singular potency as a symbol of physical fulfillment, like the lingam and yoni of Hindu sculpture—the bowstrings of the great hunter Apollo Musagetes, stretched out over the vibrant body of a woman.

As Segovia likes to tell it, the guitar was invented when Apollo was pursuing Daphne; "he embraced her, Daphne was changed into a laurel, and from the wood of the sacred tree the first guitar was made." Music historians have less romantic but equally tentative explanations. Some trace its lineage back to its namesake, the Greek *kythara*, which in turn is descended from the Chaldean *qitâra*, but neither of them has the indentation at the waist that would mark it as belonging to the true guitars, and their strings are supported by a frame rather than a neck. Other nameless instruments found on Hittite bas-reliefs and in Egyptian tombs do have proper necks and incurved sides. These, rather than the *kythara*, may have been the forerunners of the so-called Arabic *quitara*, which the conquering Moors brought to Spain during the Middle Ages, and which became so thoroughly naturalized there that it is still known as the "Spanish" guitar.

The magnificently illuminated manuscripts of the *Cantigas de Santa Maria* collected at the court of the Spanish scholar-king Alfonso the Learned show two distinct types of plucked instruments that had evolved by the middle of the thirteenth century. The *guitarra morisca*, or Moorish guitar, has an oval body, while the *guitarra latina* is distinctly pear-shaped. (Some authorities think that the term *guitarra latina*— i.e., "of the original natives"—refers to a kind of instrument already in use in western Europe before the intrusion of the Moors, but the proof of this proposition is buried somewhere in the Dark Ages.) Since neither forms nor names were standardized, succeeding centuries produced a great welter of variants: kuitra, kitra, qitara, guiterre moresche, guitarra saracenica, vihuela, vihuela de peñola, viola, quintara, quintaria, quinterne, ghiterra, ghiterma, lutina, guiterre, guiterne, kitarre, chitara, chitare, chiterra spagnuola, gitarre, and so forth.

The Spanish vihuela, or viola (originally the generic name for any stringed instrument with a neck and finger board), is not to be confused with its Italian relative, the bowed viola of the string quartet. It was an aristocratic guitar, and it was double strung like the lute, or mandolin—which is to say, its strings were arranged in courses

of two, tuned in unison or an octave apart. Vihuelas usually had six courses of strings tuned, like the lute, to *G, c, f, a', d', g'*; the more common guitar generally had the same tuning but lacked the two upper courses of strings. Then a fifth course was added to the guitar in the sixteenth century, and the pitch of the instrument was raised a tone to *A, d, g, b', e'*, which has remained the tuning of the five upper strings ever since.

The age of the vihuela was an era of great polyphonic music, and of superb virtuosos who could improvise the most elaborate counterpoint. "In my youth," writes Don Luys Zapata in his book *Miscelánea*, "there was in Valladolid a player of the vihuela called Narvaez who had such extraordinary skill that over four organ voices in a book he would instantly improvise another four —a marvel for those with no knowledge of music, and for those who understood, a great miracle."

Luis de Narvaez was one of the three major figures responsible for the flowering of the vihuela in sixteenth-century Spain. A contemporary, Luis Milan, active at the court of Queen Germaine in Valencia, was the first to break into print with his *El Maestro* of 1536, an instruction manual for those who wanted to master the vihuela. Two years later Narvaez published his *Seys Libros del Delphin de Musica* in Valladolid, and in 1546 Alonso Mudarra followed suit with his *Tres libros de Musica en cifra para vihuela*, the earliest printed book containing specific compositions for the guitar. "*Musica en cifra*" refers to the fact that the music in these volumes was not written out in staff notation but in "cipher"—number tablature similar to the symbols and diagrams used in modern guitar and ukulele editions. Instead of showing the actual notes to be sounded by the strings, the tablature symbols indicate the position of the fingers necessary to produce them.

Mudarra's collection—parts of it are played by Segovia, and all of it is avail-

able in a modern transcription—contains a magnificent cross section of what the well-equipped vihuelist was expected to know: fantasias, galliards, pavanes, *villancicos*, romances, psalms, and motets, either written by Mudarra himself or adapted from such foreign composers as Josquin and Willaert. There are settings of passages from Ovid and Virgil, and sonnets by Petrarch and Sannazaro. This is an art of high seriousness even in its dances, an art that is rhythmically very flexible and harmonically as exciting as anything written before or since.

Mudarra and more than forty other court musicians taught the nobility of Spain how to play the vihuela with ele-

Spanish classical guitarist Andrés Segovia

gance and clarity, but it remained for an amateur to write the first treatise on the common man's guitar. Juan (or Joan) Carles y Amat, author of the fifty-six-page *Guitarra Española*, was a physician and *aficionado* rather than a professional player, and he prefaces his book with an ecstatic sonnet in which his subject speaks to the reader. "You will see that I am gallant, a guardian and a guide"—

"Verás que soy galana, guarda, guia,
graciosa, gala, gracia, gallarda,
gustosa, general, grata, guitarra."

The guitar Juan Carles writes about in 1586 has only four frets and five courses of strings, but even with this relatively primitive instrument "one can play vacas, passeos, gallardas, villanos, italianas, pavanillas and similar things [the song and dance forms of the day]."

It is this eminently danceable instrument, known at home as the "Castilian" guitar, which makes its way across Europe as the *chitarra spagnuola*. The Italians become very fond of it and use it to play serenades and "*passacalli spagnoli, variati, ciacone, follie, zarabande, aire diverse, toccate musicali, balletti, correnti volte, galiarde, alemande*," as

Baroque angels serenading with lute

the title of one collection carefully itemizes. The French players of the *guiterne* are fond of *branles*, or pavanes, and later, when Robert de Visée becomes court musician to Louis XV, the winds of change bring dances like the *gavotte*, *menuet*, and *bourrée*. In Germany, however, the guitar makes little headway so long as its round-backed cousin the lute is firmly entrenched in local affections. As the baroque critic Johann Mattheson says haughtily in his *Das neueröffnete Orchester*:

"The flat guitar with its strum, strum
We shall gladly leave to the garlic-eating Spaniards."

In Britain, too, the flat-backed gittern has trouble competing with the lute except in the dance department. But both lute and guitar are found to be useful in the crucial matter of serenading the ladies. In the earliest English comedy, Nicholas Udall's *Ralph Roister Doister* (published in 1566), the hero's amatory exploits are catalogued by instruments and sound effects:

"With every woman is he in some
      love's-pang;
Then up to our lute at midnight,
      Twangledom twang!
Then twang with our sonnets, and
      twang with our dumps;
And *Heigho!* from our heart, as
      heavy as lead-lumps. . . .
Anon to our gittern, *Thrumple-dum
      thrumpledum, thrum.*"

The onomatopoeia suggests that the lute excelled as a twanger of courtly counterpoint and the guitar as a thrummer of countrified accompaniments. But the lute eventually became overloaded with strings—up to two dozen or more—which had the annoying tendency to go out of tune at the slightest provocation. If a lutenist reaches the age of eighty, Mattheson remarks, "then you can be sure that he has spent forty of his years tuning and fixing broken strings."

The sale of guitars in seventeenth-century Britain is given an immense boost by the arrival of the Italian virtuoso Francesco Corbetta at the court of Charles II. According to the *Memoirs of the Count of Gramont*, Corbetta's style "was so full of grace and tenderness that he could have given harmony to the most discordant instrument. The truth is, nothing was too difficult for this foreigner. The King's relish for his compositions had brought the instrument so much into vogue that every person played on it, well or ill; and you were as sure to see a guitar on a lady's toilet as rouge or patches."

Yet the day of hand-plucked instruments is already drawing to a close. A typical sign of the times: the Hon. Roger North, circa 1700, recommends "the harpsichord for ladies rather than the lute; one reason is, it keeps the body in a better posture than the other, which tends to make them crooked." The new-twangled quill-plucked harpsichord proves to be more convenient for playing figured basses, and "hence, away all yee lutes and guittars, and make room for the fair consort basses!" Within a generation the lute vanishes from the scene, to emerge as a museum piece two hundred years later, while the guitar retreats for a time to the inns and barbershops of Spain, where there is always one hanging from a peg for any customer in the mood to use it. Here on its native Mediterranean shore *cualquiera sabe un poco de latin y un punto en la guitarra*—everyone knows a little Latin and a chord on the guitar.

During most of the eighteenth century the fashionable world is musically otherwise occupied with the Italian opera, the beginnings of the symphony orchestra, the harpsichord, the pianoforte. When the guitar finally reappears in the drawing room it has the charm of an exotic novelty. "The instrument came to us from Italy," writes the German instrument maker August Otto. "In 1790 the Duchess Amalie of Weimar brought the first guitar from Italy to Weimar, and in those days it was regarded as a new instrument. Instantly it was warmly applauded on all sides."

Herr Otto claims that he and a Dresden conductor first had the idea of adding the low E string to the guitar, but this seems to have been another of those inventions, like the telephone, that occur to different people in different places at the same time. In any case, the guitar of 1800 was no longer an elongated, elaborately inlaid plaything; its shoulders had filled out appreciably, the curve at the waist was more pronounced, and in place of the old double courses there were now only single strings—three of gut, three of silk wound with silver wire.

The nineteenth-century romantics, who do a great deal of traveling and like to make music out of doors, learn to prize this instrument for its portability and its elastic touch. Franz Schubert's principal possessions consist of "a few books, a guitar, and a pipe"; friends who come to visit him in the mornings are accustomed to finding him still in bed, "singing newly composed songs to his guitar." Mazzini, the prophet of the Italian *Risorgimento*, goes cheerfully into exile carrying a guitar case. Thomas Moore uses a guitar to bring "The Last Rose of Summer" to the English; the pianist Moscheles notes in his diary that he has heard Moore along with Coleridge, at a party given by Sir Walter Scott's daughter, where "he sang his own poems, adapted to certain Irish melodies, harmonized and accompanied by himself on the guitar."

Upper-class England was caught up in another outburst of guitarery chiefly because Wellington's officers in the Peninsular campaigns against Napoleon had acquired a taste for it. Far from endangering the posture of young ladies, the guitar was now held to be a salubrious employment for the weaker sex. "The instrument is so obedient to the expression of their feelings—it echoes their sportive gaiety, their little griefs, calm tranquillity, and noble and elevated thoughts, with such nice precision, that it would seem to be a natural appendage and true barometer of the state of their own fair bosoms."

Despite these affinities of form and feeling, all of the serious work on the romantic guitar continued to be done by men. A whole generation of concert virtuosos, nearly all of them from Italy or Spain, established a new image of the guitar as an instrument that could, in the words of the *Westminster Review*, "warble, or articulate, or sigh, or wail, or tremble, like the human voice under emotion."

The founder of this school, Ferdinando Carulli (1770–1841), was a Neapolitan who settled in Paris. He devised a guitar with four extra bass strings (the decachord), wrote a popular *Method* that is still being reprinted, and turned out hundreds of musical works. His successor, Matteo Carcassi (1792–1853), was a Florentine who ex-

panded Carulli's technique with a *Complete Method* for the guitar which became the nineteenth century's most widely used study guide. It, too, is still in print, and has outlasted his operatic fantasias on *Zampa, William Tell*, and *Fra Diavolo*.

The best known and most influential of the Italians was the Bolognese Mauro Giuliani (1781–1828). He lived for many years in Vienna, where he helped Beethoven introduce the Battle Symphony and took part in the *Nachtmusiken* performed at the Botanical Garden by such leading musicians as Hummel, Moscheles, and Mayseder. Besides potpourris, *Ländler*, and a *Sonata Eroica*, he wrote a *Practical Method* for guitar and perfected a design of his own, the so-called *terz* guitar, which was smaller than the usual size and capable of being tuned a third higher. "Giuliani was the Paganini on his instrument," asserted the English *Giulianiad* magazine, the first real fan magazine in the annals of music. "In his hands the guitar became gifted with a power of expression at once pure, thrilling and exquisite . . . In a word, *he made the instrument sing*." (Their italics)

Giuliani's leading rival, Fernando Sor (1778–1839), was born in Barcelona but came to Britain during the Napoleonic Wars. "The Beethoven of the guitar" his admirers liked to call him. That was too tall an order: he was merely capable of turning out an occasional small masterpiece like the ones that Segovia keeps in his repertoire. But on the concert stage he made an unforgettable impression. His first recital in London "was at once magical and surprising; nobody could credit that such effects could be produced on the guitar! Indeed, there was a sort of suppressed laughter when he first came forth before the audience, which, however, soon changed into the most unbounded admiration when he began to display his talents. . . ."

This stunned reaction whenever someone happens to play the guitar really well is as repetitious as a broken

record in nineteenth-century music criticism. Virtuosity on the guitar was rather like Dr. Johnson's dog walking on his hinder legs: it was not so much how it was done, but one was surprised to find it done at all. José Maria de Ciebra, from Seville, is admired for his divine vibrato: "his guitar actually sobbed, wailed and sighed." Huerta, the ex-army officer who composed the revolutionary *Himno de Riego* (a sort of Spanish Marseillaise) is hailed in the *Revue Musicale* for having "raised the guitar to the sublime height that Paganini did the violin." Giulio Regondi, the author of yet one more obligatory *Method*, turns the guitar into

Oklahoma traveler Woody Guthrie

"quite another instrument than we have hitherto known it," as a Viennese critic observes. "He imitates by turn the violin, harp, mandolin and even the piano so naturally that you must look at him to convince yourself of the illusion." Again, not unexpectedly, "Regondi is the very Paganini of the guitar . . ."

The point of this persistent parallel is somewhat blunted by the fact that the guitar already had a Paganini, and no one else could possibly have asserted any claims to the title. Although he rose to fame on the violin, Paganini himself was also a formidable virtuoso on the guitar. Those who heard him on both instruments had difficulty deciding which one of them he played better. According to an old legend, which it would be a pity to disprove, he had spent the years from 1801 to 1804 "in absolute retirement at the chateau of a lady of high rank, devoting much time to the study of the guitar, the lady's favorite instrument." This story is corroborated by a posthumously published piece of program music for two guitars, the *Duetto Amoroso* for two lovers, dedicated to "a lady of high rank," and consisting of a rather cynical succession of nine episodes: Beginning, Entreaties, Consent, Timidity, Satisfaction (*Contentezza*), Quarrel, Peace, Love Pledges and Leave-taking. Paganini wrote almost as much music

French gypsy guitarist, 17th century

for guitar as for violin: nearly everything he published during his lifetime contains at least one guitar part.

The Marchese Massimo d'Azeglio, one of the architects of the *Risorgimento*, tells in his memoirs how he and his friends, including Paganini and Rossini, disguised themselves as singing beggars for the Roman carnival of 1821. "Rossini and Paganini were to represent the orchestra, strumming on two guitars, and thought of dressing up as women. Rossini, filled out, with great taste, his already ample contours,

stuffing them with tow, and was a really inhuman thing! Paganini, straight as a door, and with his face which resembled the handle of his violin, appeared twice as dried-up and elongated as ever. I am not inventing it, we caused a furore . . ."

Hector Berlioz, who wrote *Harold in Italy* for Paganini, says in an essay about Paganini in Paris that whenever he grew tired of playing the violin he would arrange a private séance so that he could enjoy his own string duets. "Choosing as partner a worthy German violinist, Monsieur Sina, he would take the guitar part and draw unheard-of effects from that instrument. And the two performers, Sina the unassuming violinist, and Paganini the incomparable guitarist, would thus spend together long *tête à tête* evenings to which no one, even the worthiest, ever won admittance."

Berlioz himself was a guitarist—not in Paganini's class perhaps, but from all accounts a remarkable player. He was the first important symphonist who was not at the same time a virtuoso on some more exalted instrument, such as the violin or the piano, and this singular deficiency was to have important consequences for the development of his orchestral style. During his boyhood he learned how to play only the guitar, the flute, and the flageolet. "The flute, the guitar and the flageolet!!! These are the only instruments I play, but they seem to me by no means contemptible." As a student in Paris he gave guitar lessons when the money from home ran out; as a young composer "my wretched voice and paltry guitar were often requisitioned," and when he became bored in Italy, as a winner of the Prix de Rome, he would go walking in the mountains of the Abruzzi, guitar in hand, "strolling along, shouting or singing, careless as to where I should sleep."

Sometimes Berlioz would amuse the peasants along the way by playing saltarellos till his fingers burned. "I make them happy with my guitar," he writes

to a friend in September, 1831. "Before I came they only danced to the tambour de basque, and they are delighted with this melodious instrument." He writes in his memoirs that when he was alone with his guitar he would remember long-forgotten passages from Virgil's *Aeneid*. "Then, improvising a strange recitative to a still stranger harmony, I would sing the death of Pallas, the despair of the good Evander, of his horse Ethon, unharnessed and with flowing mane and falling tears, following the young warrior's corpse to its last resting-place . . . This combination of memories, poetry and music used to work me into the most incredible state of excitement; and the triple intoxication generally culminated in torrents of tears."

This is as fine a picture as any we possess of the musical creative process as the romantics understood it. On these hot afternoons above Subiaco he was laying the groundwork for his great Virgilian music-drama, *The Trojans*. And he was not exaggerating when he claimed that the whole of the *Aeneid* had come pouring out of the sound hole of his guitar. Berlioz accompanying himself was equivalent to a whole opera company. His friend Ernest Legouvé, the French playwright, once heard him sing the second act of Spontini's *La Vestale* to his guitar and was stirred to comment:

"He sang everything—the high priest, the vestals, Julia—all the characters, all the parts. *Malheureusement*, he did not have a voice. No matter; he made one. Thanks to a method of singing with a closed mouth which he used with extraordinary skill, thanks to the passion and musical genius that animated him, he drew from his chest, his throat and his guitar unknown sounds, piercing lamentations, which—occasionally mingled with cries of admiration and enthusiasm, even eloquent commentaries—united to produce a total effect that was such an incredible whirlwind of verve and passion that no performance of this opera has moved me . . . so much as did this singer without a voice, and his guitar."

The natural enemy of this kind of music making was the grand piano. A nineteenth-century piano was not so much an instrument as a vested interest, as immobile as a piece of real estate. It was a triumph of mechanical engineering—a thing of levers and bolts and hammers, utterly insensitive to the difference between being struck by a maiden's finger or the end of an umbrella. Against this massive machine and its minions a small hand-plucked box can make little headway, and in the second half of the century the guitar is once again driven from polite society and relegated to the saltimbanques and garlic eaters.

In the days of Victorian opulence the best place to find guitars is in their native country, and it is to Spain that the French and Russian composers now come, impelled by an awakening interest in folk music, to observe the guitar in its natural habitat for the first time. When the aristocratic Mikhail Glinka, the founder of the Russian national school, visited Andalusia at mid-century, he spent hours and days listening to the fandangos of Francisco Rodriguez, El Murciano, who was the finest guitarist in Granada. "This Murciano was a simple, untutored person who traded in wine at his own tavern," says Glinka in his memoirs. "He played the guitar with uncommon skill, however, and with great precision. . . ." A few years earlier the first of Granada's *cafés cantantes* had opened their doors, and the gypsy musicians hired to play in them developed increasingly dazzling ways of attracting customers. Emmanuel Chabrier, a Parisian to his fingertips, is slightly overwhelmed to find a Spanish way of life predicated on two guitars, five or six dancing gypsies, and a cask of manzanilla sherry. After a run of nights watching the *malagueñas*, *soledas*, and *zapateados*, he writes from Granada to a friend at home:

"If you saw them wriggling their behinds, swaying their hips and twisting their bodies you wouldn't want to be off in a hurry. At Malaga things got so hot that I had to take my wife away; that was a bit too much . . . This is what happens: one or two women begin dancing, two queer chaps scrape something on tinny guitars and five or six women bawl out in a screamingly funny voice triplets which are impossible to note down for they keep changing the tune . . . You hear syllables, words, portamentos, then they begin clapping and beating out the six eighth-notes, accentuating the third and sixth; and then come the shouts: '*Anda, anda! La Salud! Anda, anda! Consuelo! Olé, la Lola! Olé, la Carmen! Que gracia, que elegancia!*' all this designed to excite the dancing girls—it's simply staggering."

The flamenco guitar sounds tinny to foreigners because it is smaller and lighter than the classic Spanish guitar; cypress, maple, or walnut are used instead of rosewood and the head is kept light for balance, since the flamenco style requires that the instrument be held nearly upright, resting on the right thigh. More recently the flamenco guitar has also acquired plastic tapping plates (anathema to the classical player), designed to protect the wood against the thousand daily drum taps that turn it into a percussion instrument, and against the side effects of the constant *rasgueado*—the swift rasping or scraping of the strings which is the hallmark of Andalusian guitarists.

In the *cante jondo*, the famous "deep song" of Andalusia, the guitar traditionally plays a subordinate role and is supposed to limit itself to marking the rhythm and following the *cante*. "It is a foundation for the voice and should be subjected to the will of the singer," as Federico García Lorca says in one of his lectures on the art of flamenco. "But since the personality of the guitarist is as deeply involved as that of the singer, he too must sing out, and thus *falsetas* [guitar improvisations] are born, which are the commentaries of the strings, sometimes of extraordinary beauty . . ."

The great flamenco guitarists—men like Paco El Barbero ("The Barber"), El Maestro Patiño, and Habichuela ("Kidney Bean")—not only knew how to play dazzling *falsetas* but were able to sing or dance all of the *cantes* and *bailes* they played for. Within the present framework of flamenco there are perhaps fifty distinct ways of singing and thirty styles of dancing—*alegrías, caracoles, chuflas, fandanguillos, jaleos, polos, romeras, siguiriyas, soleares, zambras,* and so on. There are also thirty or so kinds of solo playing, but the guitarist who appears only as a soloist is a relatively recent development, viewed with suspicion by *aficio-*

Blues man "Leadbelly" with 12-string guitar

nados like Lorca, who knew flamenco before it was commercialized. For Lorca, the guitar was a *corazón malherido por cinco espadas*, a "heart grievously wounded by five swords," as he says in his poem *"La Guitarra,"* from which this excerpt is taken:

*"Se rompen las copas
de la madrugada.
Empieza el llanto
de la guitarra.
Es inútil callarla.
Es imposible
callarla.*

Llora monótona
como llora el agua,
como llora el viento
sobre la nevada. . . ."

"The wine cups of daybreak
are shattered.
The lament
of the guitar begins.
It is useless to silence it.
It is impossible
to silence it.
It weeps monotonously
as the water weeps,
as the wind weeps
over the snowfall. . . ."

French music party with lute, 17th century

There is only one other guitar that shatters the wine cups of daybreak—the blues guitar of the American Negro. They may seem far removed in geography and tradition, but there is, indeed, a historical connection between the two. The West African Negroes who were brought to America in slave ships were accustomed to playing many of the same twanging instruments as the Moors and Berbers north of the Sahara. And although these Negroes were usually forbidden to play their tribal drums in America for fear of slave insurrections, they were encouraged to go on making and playing their stringed instruments.

Thomas Jefferson writes of the slaves in his *Notes on Virginia*: "The instrument proper to them is the Banjar, which they brought hither from Africa, and which is the original of the guitar, its chords [strings] being precisely the four lower chords of the guitar." This skin-covered gourd instrument was the West African *bania*, soon to become better known as the banjo and henceforth indispensable to a dozen kinds of American music. Jefferson was correct in supposing a relationship between the banjo and the guitar, but one is not descended from the other; according to the best available evidence, both are collateral descendants of the Moorish *quitara*.

In America, where musical integration is a continuous process going back to colonial times, the banjo player from Africa meets the guitar player from Europe, and the result is that instruments as well as styles are exchanged. The white forty-niner goes off to California with the banjo on his knee, and the Negro singer addresses his *cante jondo* to the guitar: "Sometimes I feel like nothin'; sometimes th'owed away;/Then I get my guitar and play the blues all day . . ." For singers like Blind Lemon Jefferson and Big Bill Broonzy there is something tactile and responsive about the guitar that makes it the ideal blues instrument—something a piano could never achieve with its eighty-eight-note span.

The guitar has gradually become an essential part of the whole *Top of Old Smoky*–Joan Baez school of folk singing in America. Historically, however, it is a late-comer to the ballad style, and the standard guitar accompaniments to "The Foggy Dew" and such are merely modern additions to Elizabethan originals. The English ballads that form the substratum of American folk song were traditionally sung unaccompanied, and "not only without gestures but with the greatest restraint in the matter of expression," according to the pioneer song hunter Cecil Sharp. "Indeed, the folk singer will usually close his eyes and observe an impassive demeanor throughout his performance." On the American frontier these same songs first acquired accompaniments on instruments like the dulcimer, introduced by German settlers, and the parson's fiddle. Guitars appeared on the scene from three directions: the East Coast cities that followed London trends in drawing-room music (Benjamin Franklin was a salon guitarist); the Spanish Southwest, where songs were always accompanied on the guitar, and few adobes were without one; and the Negro South.

In many areas it was the Negro influence that proved to be decisive. The same hillbillies who now seem as inseparable from their guitars as Siamese twins were still singing to their dulcimers, or unaccompanied, in the 1900's. "Negroes introduced the guitar and the blues into the hills some time after the turn of the century," writes Alan Lomax, "so recently in fact that the most complex of hillbilly guitar styles is still called 'nigger pickin'.'" The average Arkansas traveler and folk guitarist, however, is satisfied with something far less sophisticated. "I learned that I could plunk along on 'Birmingham Jail' in the key of, say, G and get by plumb and dandy with only one chord change in the whole song, up to D and back to greasy G," says Woody Guthrie. "Lots of the old full-blooded fiddlers will toss you down off from his platform if you go to getting too fancy with your chording."

The musical wheel came full circle when enterprising Liverpudlians wedded the hillbilly guitar to their own British music-hall tradition to produce the so-called Mersey beat, which requires at least three guitars to make itself heard above the surrounding percussion: lead guitar, rhythm guitar, and bass guitar. These Anglo-Ozark instruments, however, are usually ignoble and amoebic in shape. Electronically amplified to raise their Janizary twang to the nth power for purposes of profit, they have patented reverberation-intensity control units, Bigsby vibratos, mute levers, chrome-plated tuning keys, nickel-plated silver frets, and celluloid-bound oval finger-boards. In name only can they be regarded as offspring of the great Persian guitar which Ziryab, the pupil of Ishaq at the court of Harun-al-Rashid in Baghdad, brought to Cordova in the enlightened reign of the Emir Abd al-Rahman II.

Meanwhile, the unamplified, which is to say the classic, guitar of Sor and Giuliani has lacked neither apostles nor audiences of its own. The great Spanish revival began before the turn of the century with Francisco Tárrega, an artist of almost legendary powers who played in the streets as a boy and then became an immensely influential teacher in Barcelona. "San Francisco Tárrega," as Segovia calls him, awakened the latent possibilities of the concert guitar by writing a new romantic repertoire for it, and by making more than a hundred transcriptions from Beethoven, Chopin, Schumann, Bach. The terms of musical reference had changed by then: critics refer to him as the Sarasate and the Anton Rubinstein of the guitar. "In his hands," reported a Madrid critic, "the guitar cries and laughs. Sometimes it sounds like a harp, other times like a whole orchestra of *bandurrias* (the Spanish mandolin). When he plays a *jota* we seem to hear the words of the *coplas*; no doubt he has a *duende* [familiar spirit] which sings inside the guitar." And Isaac Albéniz said, when he heard Tárrega perform one of his piano pieces in a guitar transcription: "This is just as I had conceived it . . ."

After Tárrega's death in 1909, at the age of fifty-seven, his work was carried on by a circle of gifted pupils, including Miguel Llobet, Alberto Obregón, and Emilio Pujol. Llobet was known for many years as the most elegant guitarist in Spain; he gave concerts throughout Europe as well as in South America and the United States, but during the Spanish Civil War, at the height of his career, he died in the besieged city of Barcelona. Tárrega, Llobet, Pujol, and half a dozen others are the reason that the modern guitar

revival did not have to spring fully armed from the forehead of Andrés Segovia, as is sometimes assumed. But it remained for Segovia to reap what the others had sown and to establish a sovereign place for the guitar in the twentieth century's arsenal of new and exciting sounds.

Segovia, born in Linares in southern Spain in February 1894, came north too late to have the benefit of Tárrega's teaching. He is, in fact, as completely self-taught as it is possible for a musician to be, and by his own account, "as I had to fight the opposition of my family there was no question of a teacher, a school, or any other of the usual methods of instruction." He taught himself how to play from books, including Tárrega's; he plays Tárrega's studies superlatively, and he sees himself as pursuing the same fundamental goal of expanding the horizons and repertoire of the guitar.

"Segovia is the Cortot of the guitar," writes the French critic Bernard Gavoty. It might be more accurate— using this formula just once more—to call him the Landowska of the guitar, for like the rediscoverer of the harpsichord he is virtually the sole proprietor of certain vast tracts of musical estate. The twenty-one LP records that he has made for Decca thus far merely sketch in the outlines of Segovia's private demesne; it includes vihuelists like Milan and Mudarra, the gallant music of Visée, romantic works by Sor and Paganini, and pieces by modern masters, like the incomparable *Homenaje* which Manuel de Falla wrote *pour le tombeau de Debussy*. His transcriptions of Handel and Bach have ceased to horrify the purists, for it is now generally conceded that a work like the immense Bach *Chaconne* sounds far more natural and effective on the guitar than it ever did on the solo violin.

When Segovia made his debut in Paris in 1924, Albert Roussel presented him with a special concert piece—it was called *Segovia*—and since then he

has encouraged many other composers to think in terms of the guitar. In effect a whole department of musical literature has been created, like Joan Manén's *Fantasia-Sonata*, especially "*por y para Andrés Segovia*." At the same time, his presence and example have opened doors for a great many other virtuoso guitarists: Rey de la Torre, Julian Bream, Julio Martínez Oyanguren, Narciso Yepes, Laurindo Almeida, John Williams, Karl Scheit. It is Segovia who has established the criteria by which every young guitarist must measure himself, and it was he who accustomed international audiences to

Greenwich Village folk-sing: Odetta and fans

the idea that one could spend two hours in a concert hall listening to a man playing the guitar.

Segovia does not play like an orchestra; his instrument moans not, neither does it wail. It is at all times nothing more nor less than a transcendently well-played guitar—an honest and affecting sound because it is a beautifully handmade thing, in which the left hand always knows what the right hand is doing. And that, in the last analysis, is the point and purpose of the whole art of the Apollonian twang.

Frederick V. Grunfeld is a well-known music critic. A world traveler and an avid collector of primitive art, he now lives on the island of Majorca in Spain.

IOHANNES BUCHOLDI A LEYDA

Besieged in their "holy city" of Mün-ster (at right, surrounded by a moat), the Anabaptists fought the mounting forces of much of the old Holy Roman Empire for sixteen months. When the walled bastion of the revolutionaries fell, their prophet Jan of Leyden (at left, pointing to a page of the Old Tes-tament) was caught, tortured to death, and strung up in a cage hanging from the tower of St. Lambert's Church. The sketch at right, and those on the following two pages, were done by Er-hard Schoen, an artist of the time.

THE HOLY TERRORS OF MUNSTER

**They were the Anabaptists—the lunatic fringe
of the sixteenth century—and
they staged a revolution that anticipated the
"psychic epidemics" of our own time**

In the long record of man's savagery to man, there can be no more brutal episode than the drama of the Ana-baptist revolution played out in the small city of Münster in northwest Germany in 1534–35. There, as the medieval world was dying and the modern age dawning, as an ancient social order disintegrated and a new proletariat was born, starving and des-perate men conceived a utopian king-dom of eternal goodness and eternal peace—and ended by creating a fore-runner of the modern totalitarian state.

Anticipating the French Revolution by more than two hundred and fifty years, and the Nazis and the Commu-nists by nearly four hundred, the Ana-baptist revolution in Münster was strik-ing in its modernities of class warfare,

thought control, communal farms, an elite military corps, and a proto-Ges-tapo. The Anabaptist leaders were brutal fanatics: believing that the world was an abomination of corrup-tion, they were determined to destroy it. "The glory of all the Saints," they asserted, "is to wreak vengeance. . . . Revenge without mercy is the fate of all who are not marked with the Sign."

Within the walls of the city, Jan of Leyden had proclaimed himself the Anabaptist king and messiah. Deter-mined to destroy the institutions of private property and marriage, he pre-sided over a mounting orgy of political terror and sexual license. Sitting in the market place, surrounded by two hun-dred courtiers and fifteen wives, he passed judgment on traitors, appeas-

ers, and the merely weak-willed, whom he beheaded with his own sword.

Outside the city gathered all the forces of the Holy Roman Empire, Catholic and Protestant alike. Acting to protect privilege and what they con-ceived to be God's true order, they buried their doctrinal differences in a counterrevolutionary alliance and pledged to extirpate the Holy City of the Anabaptists by death and fire. In the end they succeeded, but not until they had matched atrocity for atrocity in the sixteen-month siege of Münster.

In some sense Martin Luther had started it all, though the Anabaptist heresy—as all rebellion—was repug-nant to him. "Rebellion brings with it a land full of murder," he wrote in 1525, condemning those who under-

By EDMUND STILLMAN

mined the secular order. "Let everyone who can, smite, slay, and stab . . . remembering that nothing can be more poisonous, hurtful, or devilish than a rebel."

Luther had dreamed of a *spiritual* freedom. In his view the earthly order was trivial, a mere anteroom to Paradise and Hell. It was also sacrosanct, since disorder was the Devil's work. What Luther could not see was that the medieval structure of belief he helped to bring tumbling down was a marvelously intricate web of social relations in which lord, priest, artisan, and peasant had, for something like a thousand years, functioned in close interrelationship. Medieval man shivered in the cold and was lucky if he died peacefully of the fever, in his bed; but unlike today's rootless and alienated men, medieval man did not doubt his place in the scheme of things. To question the medieval dogmas was tantamount to questioning everything, and so to open the floodgates of doubt.

Lutherans might care only for the question of man's relationship to God. But men could not question that relationship without questioning the secular law as well—simply because few men had learned to distinguish between the two. In the process of revolutionary questioning, the Anabaptists were a phenomenon that has become familiar in our own time. They were the lunatic fringe or, perhaps more fairly, they were the radical left wing of those many others who sought a new Godly dispensation in the world.

That the old social order was corrupt, few serious men denied. Rome, where a few years earlier a Borgia had managed to attain the throne of Saint Peter, was a scandal. In 1490, according to the great historian Henri Pirenne, there were at least 6,800 courtesans in the Holy City. The pope and his cardinals "consorted publicly with their mistresses, acknowledged their bastards," Pirenne says, and endowed them with riches stolen from the coffers of the Church. The conduct of the clergy outside Rome was hardly better, as Erasmus and Sir Thomas More, men who died faithful to their church, repeatedly pointed out.

But the state of the Church alone does not account for the turmoil that convulsed the sixteenth century. As the

91

Firing from their battlements, Münsterites hold the attackers at bay

Dangerous social unrest in Germany dated back to the early years of the century. The early sporadic peasant risings against the feudal lords had been largely conservative in character. Even the Great Peasants' War of 1524–25, which aroused Luther's fury and in which one hundred thousand died, impresses us today with the reasonableness of its demands. But when the peasant uprising was crushed, the vision of God's kingdom on earth went underground, ready to burst forth with greater violence once again.

Anabaptism began, at about this time, as a purely religious movement in opposition to conservative Lutheranism. Its name means, in Greek, "to baptize again," and its basic doctrine was that infant baptism did not suffice to make a man a Christian. As Anabaptism developed, however, it was transformed into a genuine revolutionary movement of the poor and disinherited who broke with Lutheranism because they saw in it a bulwark of the authority of the princes.

Caring little for theological speculation, the followers of Anabaptism read their Bibles literally and with total commitment, and riveted their attention on the social doctrines of the Gospels: to the poor belonged the earth and eternal life. Private property was at best a hindrance to salvation; and the extremists among the Anabaptists believed that communal ownership was God's order for the world.

century began, an old way of life was passing in the northwest of Europe: put simply, it was the death of the old, static, agrarian, traditional culture and the birth of a new, urban, commercial, capitalist, and proto-industrial civilization which has led down, in an unbroken line since then, to our own.

Lewis Mumford has called the sixteenth century the dawn age of technology—the "Eotechnic Age." Vast technological improvements were either invented or put into widespread operation in that century—Among them the blast furnace, artillery, the printing press, the power loom, the domestic clock, and cheap paper for books. The initial effect of such devices was not simply to improve life but to contort it: the new inventions spurred the growth of factories and created a new, rootless industrial proletariat siphoned off from the once stable peasant communities of the countryside.

The capitalism of sixteenth-century Europe was naked, entrepreneurial capitalism, unchecked by social conscience or the intervention of governments—which, in any case, were too weak to govern the burgeoning new industries. And as industrialism grew and the old order died, the whole peasant world was shaken. Inflation, over-population, and repeated bad harvests and plagues reduced the peasants of Germany and The Netherlands to a misery they had rarely known.

In such circumstances the old tradition of the last days revived. Men began to see in their afflictions the coming of the Biblical "Apocalypse"—the reign of Antichrist to be succeeded by a perfect peace on earth wherein men would dwell in harmony with one another. Thus, the men who followed Jan of Leyden in his brutal effort to take the millennium by frontal assault were not comfortable burghers, artisans, and peasants secure in their place in society. They were not men tightly integrated into the old system of city guilds and manorial farms. They were landless peasants, or peasants with too little land; they were beggars and unskilled workmen, on the fringes of society. They were the abandoned, the desperate, and the afraid—in short, the stuff of which every fanatic movement of modern times has been made.

Soldiers of the prince-bishop lie dead among the advanced earthworks

Cannon and a mortar (right) fire on the town from behind wicker gabions

The princes hunted down the Anabaptists by the thousands, but in doing so, only intensified the Anabaptists' fanatical belief in the imminent coming of the Earthly Kingdom. Like revolutionaries before and since, the Anabaptists were divided into pacifist and militant wings, and from the princes' point of view, the worst feature of the persecutions was that they tended to kill off the peaceful Anabaptists and drive the movement more and more into the hands of those who wanted to take the Earthly Kingdom by blood and fire.

Münster in the sixteenth century was that anomaly of the jerry-built Holy Roman Empire, a petty ecclesiastical state ruled by a bishop who was at the same time a prince. In the state of Münster the privileged clergy were everything, and there were many of them: the tiny prince-bishopric boasted four monasteries, seven convents, ten churches, and a cathedral, each with its vast bureaucracy. Throughout the principality, monks carried on a thriving commerce outside the jurisdiction of the guild. Virtually all the clergy were exempt from taxation. Thus the real public burden was carried by a struggling merchant middle class, by artisans who bitterly resented the competition of the monks (who, they charged, supported no families, paid no taxes, and did no military service), and by the wretched Münster proletariat, who had three times between 1498 and 1522 been

forced to contribute a sizable donation to the Roman Curia when a new Bishop was elected. By 1534, to make matters worse, the prince-bishop was not even a true priest but a secular lord who had not taken the trouble to be ordained.

Against this background of general misery and discontent, as Norman Cohn has pointed out in his excellent study *The Pursuit of the Millennium*, one disaster followed another: in 1529 an outbreak of the Black Death ravaged Westphalia; the crops failed; warfare in the Baltic closed the ports and prevented the importation of grain. Between 1529 and 1530 the price of rye, the poor man's staple, rose by 300 per cent. In 1530 the prince-bishop sought to *sell* his bishopric to the Bishop of Paderborn. Two years later,

the town opted for Lutheranism and drove out its priests.

But Münster would not remain Lutheran, and conservative, for long. When, in 1532, the nearby Duchy of Cleves expelled its Anabaptists, many of them migrated to Münster, carrying with them their doctrinal contagion. From then on the movement grew within the walls of the city. In 1533 new recruits, the first of many, arrived from The Netherlands, among them Jan Bockelson of Leyden, a young man of twenty-four who had been baptized into the movement only a few months before. "And so they came," records a chronicle, "the Dutch and the Frisians and the scoundrels from all parts who had never settled anywhere: they flocked to Münster and collected there." And these new arrivals called attention to a startling fact: the year 1533, in their eschatology, was the fifteenth centenary of the Passion of Christ. The last days of the world, the Anabaptists declared, were now at hand.

About the same time, as Cohn says, an elderly baker from Haarlem named Matthys had succeeded to the mantle of the Anabaptist prophets; but unlike his peaceful predecessors Matthys preached that the millennium demanded blood. From Haarlem he sent out his "apostles" to preach the doctrine of the imminent Coming and of rebellion against the princes of this world. He watched the rising fever in Münster. In February, 1534, he followed his young

Waiting for the barrage to lift, infantry assemble for the final assault

disciple, Jan of Leyden, to the city and proceeded to take control.

In its feverish state the city was helpless before him. Street crowds ruled the town, their numbers increased by the immigrants. A further cause of hysteria came from the hundreds of nuns who had broken their vows, put on secular dress, and accepted baptism in the new faith preached by Matthys.

The Anabaptists seized the town hall and the market place. The town council, Protestant in its sympathies, hesitated to use force, and the result was a compromise. The Anabaptists won legal recognition, but in the uncertain atmosphere of the town the conservative elements began to flee. By early 1534 the fanatical sectarians made up the majority of the population. In leaflets exhorting neighboring towns they warned that the earth was doomed; by Easter it would be destroyed. But Münster, that New Jerusalem, that new Ark, would be saved. All who desired salvation were to come to the city. They were to come bringing arms.

The result of these hysterical appeals was a new influx of believers, from parts as distant as Brabant in southern Holland. On February 23, 1534, in a new election of the town council, the Anabaptists won a decisive victory. The first official move of the once-persecuted sect was to expel the remaining Catholics and Lutherans—all of them destitute, many of them half-naked in the dead of the German winter. Those who remained underwent mass baptisms in the market place. By March there were no "disciples of the Devil" left in Münster. Addressing one another as "Brother" and "Sister," preaching perfect communal love, the Anabaptists made both Catholicism and Lutheranism capital offenses.

From his residence outside the town, the reigning prince-bishop, Franz von Waldeck, had uneasily watched the progress of the doctrinal revolution within his city. He had tolerated the conservative Lutheran burghers; but

now as the social revolution began, he determined to crush it. Anticipating a war, the Anabaptists in their turn established a regular army, appointed officers of the watch, manned the walls, emplaced cannon, and dug earthworks to strengthen the town's defenses. Every man and woman within the walls was conscripted. The property of the exiles was confiscated; and each Anabaptist family was assigned, according to its need, a patch of communal land. All account books and promissory notes found among the effects of the exiles were burned. What was wearable or edible was taken into a central storehouse to be distributed by seven "deacons." "The poorest amongst us, who used to be despised as beggars, now go about dressed as finely as the highest and most distinguished," boasted an Anabaptist leaflet. "By God's grace they [the despised] have become as rich as the burgomasters. . ."

When at last the prince-bishop's forces moved in to begin the siege of Münster, the Dutch extremists instituted a reign of "justice and virtue." For two months there was unremitting propaganda against private ownership and capital. The surrender of private wealth to the public stores was made a test of Christian faith. Once the money was seized, it was used only for public purposes—for the hiring of mercenaries to bolster the town's defenses and for the purchase of needed stores. Workers within the town received their wages in kind. "Amongst us," an Anabaptist wrote, "God . . . has restored community as it was in the beginning and as befits the Saints of God. . . . And accordingly, everything which has served the purposes of self seeking and private property, such as buying and selling, working for money, taking interest and practicing usury . . . or eating and drinking the sweat of the poor . . . all such things are abolished amongst us by the power of love . . . ."

In the meantime the authorities of the bishopric and neighboring principalities of Cleves and Cologne cordoned off the city. Cavalry patrolled

the roads into Münster and all traffic to and fro was halted. In April, 1534, Matthys made a sortie against the prince-bishop's forces. He moved against the great army with only a dozen men, acting, he alleged, on a vision sent him by God, and believing himself to be invincible. He was instantly captured and butchered by the prince-bishop's men.

The movement might have collapsed with the death of the prophet, but his disciple, Jan of Leyden, now came forward, revealing new qualities of leadership. Haranguing the crowds, he restored their faith in victory, and military operations continued. In May, running naked through the streets, Jan fell into a trance. When he awoke, he proclaimed *his* great vision: Jan of Leyden was to reign as king in God's new Israel, assisted by a council of Twelve Elders.

The messianic kingdom was now established, and a new legal code eliminated nearly every vestige of private property. But it was in the realm of sexual behavior that Jan of Leyden now moved to legislate. God, he asserted, had required of men that they increase and multiply. Like the patriarchs of Israel, the Anabaptists of Münster were to take many wives: there was a surplus of women in the town—spoiled nuns and the widows of the slain. Once again, those who demurred were executed. (There is no record in any case that the new legislation caused much grief to these derelict and desperate women, though under the system of strict sexual subordination they had little opportunity to speak.) For a woman to complain of plural marriage became, like so much else in this new kingdom, a capital offense.

Jan of Leyden himself took fifteen wives—the most beautiful of them Divara, the widow of the old prophet Matthys. The king set up his court in the old palace of the bishops and dressed himself—as a symbol of God's magnificence—in silks and gold.

At the same time he did not entirely neglect the war. By summer two hundred of the prince-bishop's mercenaries had gone over to the Anabaptists. In an attack on the walls at the end of August, 1534, the bishop's forces were repulsed—and disintegrated. For the moment it seemed that Münster was reprieved.

Alas for Münster, the victory went to the head of the Anabaptist king. Perhaps he really believed that God had already sent salvation to the faithful and that new victories were in store. In any event, rather than flee the besieged city, Jan of Leyden maintained his profligate court, played at theatricals, and legislated a new social order that grew more and more bizarre.

Jan proclaimed himself king of all the world. His elite troops wore emblems of a globe pierced by two swords—the sword of Faith and the sword of secular Power. His throne was draped with cloth of gold. Beside him stood two pages—one bearing a copy of the Old Testament and the other a sword. The court played and feasted through the night. Meanwhile, the common people were worked in a regimen of tireless austerity, as the king's councilor suddenly announced that God hated all excess of dress. Eighty-three wagonloads of clothing and bedding were collected for the central stores.

The town grew more and more debauched; the defenses were neglected—and the prince-bishop returned to the attack. The town was doomed when, in April, 1535, at an Imperial Diet at Worms all the states of the Holy Roman Empire voted to contribute money and forces to the siege. Münster was completely isolated from aid by an elaborate ring of "trenches and blockhouses, and by a double line of infantry and cavalry," so that even the expected Anabaptist relief forces from Holland and north Germany could not hope to break through. As the people of Münster starved, the king ordered dances in the market square. He first promised military deliverance by foreign allies, and when that was seen to be futile, he promised a divine salvation. God the Father, he proclaimed, would change the cobblestones to bread. Men wept when the cobblestones remained stone. By late spring every animal in the town had been killed and eaten. Men gnawed at pieces of leather, and at "the bodies of the dead."

Soon the only relief from horror was sexual. Having abolished monogamy and proclaimed plural marriage early in his divine reign, Jan presided over a protracted orgy. All notions of family broke down. Men and women coupled freely, joining and parting each day, not caring any longer even for the forms of authorized communal marriage. Even that, it seemed to the populace, presupposed permanence in a world of terrifying impermanency. In this, too, the king was an example to his people: he could not sin, he proclaimed, because he was "wholly dead to the world."

"At last, in May [1535], when most of the inhabitants had tasted no bread for eight weeks," writes Cohn, "the king agreed that those who wished should leave the town. Even then he cursed the fugitives, promising them that the reward for their infidelity would be everlasting damnation. Their earthly fate was indeed fearful enough. The able-bodied men were at once put to the sword; as for the women and old men and children, the Bishop feared—not unreasonably—that if they passed through his lines they would stir up trouble in the rear and accordingly refused to allow them past the blockhouses. These people therefore lingered on for five long weeks in the no man's land before the town walls, begging the mercenaries to kill them, crawling about and eating grass like animals and dying in such numbers that the ground was littered with corpses."

Within the city the Anabaptists watched from the walls and jeered, acting out the belief so dear to medieval man that the greatest delight of the saved in Paradise was watching the sufferings of the damned in Hell.

In the end it was the king's brutality in driving the misbelievers from the city that destroyed him. On the night of June 24, 1535, one of the starving expellees crawling about between the siege works and the town walls offered to show the prince-bishop's troops a secret entry into the city. An assault breached the town's defenses. By morning the town had fallen. About three hundred Anabaptist troops surrendered on promise of their lives, only to be slaughtered almost to a man.

The end of Jan of Leyden was grimmer still. Captured by the bishop, he was led about the Empire for a time, exhibited on a chain. In January, 1536, he was returned to Münster, branded and clawed by pincers, and forced to sit on a blazing iron throne.

The bishop's power and the Catholic faith were restored in Münster. Everything was as before. Until this century, the bones of Jan of Leyden swung in their cage from the tower of the Church of St. Lambert's in Münster. The Anabaptist movement, in its militant wing, was stamped out. The direct survivors of the Anabaptists today are the peaceful Mennonites and Amish of the Pennsylvania countryside.

But the impulse that drove the Anabaptists to rebellion did not die. The vision of the Earthly Kingdom of justice, and the tradition of taking the millennium by assault, survived underground—among the poor, desperate, and degraded, wherever one social order died and a new one struggled for birth. Indeed the story of the Anabaptists of Münster is an antecedent of what Carl Jung has called the "psychic epidemics of our time."

Edmund Stillman, an Associate of the Hudson Institute, wrote a profile of Konrad Lorenz for the Spring HORIZON.

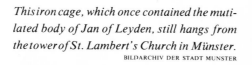

This iron cage, which once contained the mutilated body of Jan of Leyden, still hangs from the tower of St. Lambert's Church in Münster.
BILDARCHIV DER STADT MUNSTER

THE DANCE

A GRAVURE PORTFOLIO OF PHOTOGRAPHS
BY HERBERT MIGDOLL

The rhythms and movements of the dance—from classical ballet to the most colloquial of dances—have always held a special fascination for photographers. They provide an opportunity to play with time—to arrest a moment, or prolong it, to freeze and suspend a gesture, or blur it into a continuous flow of movement.

Recently, a thirty-year-old photographer named Herbert Migdoll, working with high-speed color film, raised dance photography to a new artistic level. His time and motion studies of the dancer at work, reproduced in this gravure portfolio, are undeniably poetic statements in their own right.

In the history of the dance, this is an era of exciting technical experiment. Forms that seem to have existed for little more than a few years are now "traditional," and traditions are being scrapped and abandoned with glee.

Martha Graham, yesterday's rebel, is today's tradition, and she is one of the few of the old guard still held in esteem by young adventurers. Miss Graham has completed the work begun by Isadora Duncan—carrying to its conclusion the rebellion against the stereotyped and stylized forms of classical ballet. Indeed, she was the first to create a style of "angularity and dissonance" that we now recognize as the very essence of "modern" dance and ballet.

If Martha Graham is responsible for much of the modern dance we see today (performed by her own rebellious pupils and partners, like Merce Cunningham, Erick Hawkins, Paul Taylor, and Anna Sokolow), she has also created a new climate for experiment in the classical ballet. And, to this extent, George Balanchine is in her debt. Balanchine, in his spectacular story ballets, still has one foot in the nineteenth century, but his most important works today are those that have no story line at all—those that are abstract, generally impersonal orchestrations of movement for its own dramatic sake.

In a climate, then, that enthusiastically (not to say compulsively)

CONTINUED ON PAGE 105

Captions for the photographs appear on page 105.

1

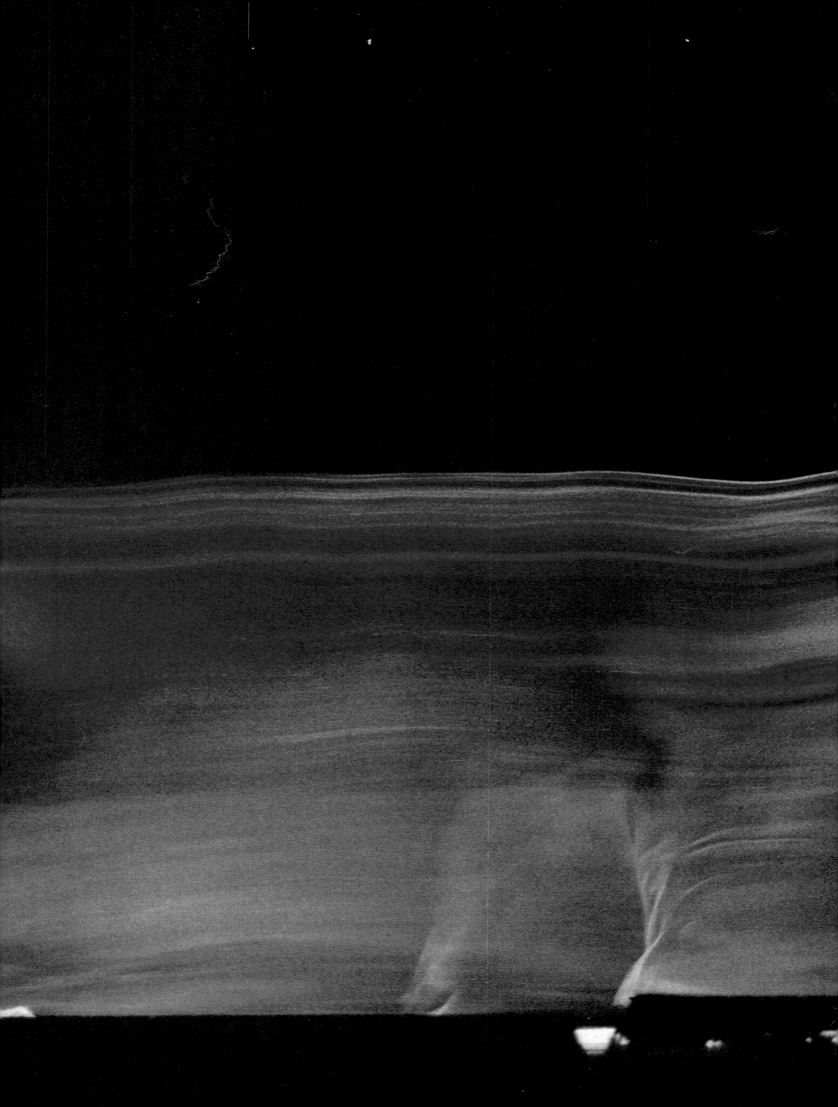

CONTINUED FROM PAGE 96

questioned the values of the past, the dancers of the past two decades have set out to prove that anything is possible. Alwin Nikolais, whose presentations of movement, sound, and light are reminiscent of the experiments of the Bauhaus, offers an experience that rests solely on the effect of depersonalized bodies moving in harmony with personalized props and costumes. At its best, his nonliteral dance is pure theatrical magic.

The most avant of the avant-garde declared war on meaning itself. Eschewing poetically coherent dance of any sort, they turned first to the surprise and shock of the Dance of the Absurd and, more recently, to happenings—in which it is, admittedly, difficult to distinguish between creative expression and mere exercise.

Sheer theatricality links Nikolais's shapes with the Polish Mime Theatre. Its reliance on striking rhythmic movement, on simple and yet evocative images, and its mixing of media—abstract dance forms and dramatic narrative co-exist—may lead to a new modern-dance form and create the ultimate in "total theatre."

In the meantime, removed from all these warring aesthetics, folk dance has also been revivified in the past two decades by professional choreographers. From the Moiseyev Dance Company to the Ballet Folklórico de México, from the Bayanihan dancers of the Philippines to Les Ballet Africains, folk ballets have captured audiences throughout the country.

If folk dance seems more congenial than many of the other styles of dance current today, it may be for the simplest of reasons: its forms were created for the sake of dancing, not for the sake of experimenting. And, if one can make any pronouncement about the future of the dance, it may be that the tumultuousness of the experimentation is over; dancers may soon turn from the exploration of technique to the expressive use of the techniques they have. They may, in short, stop experimenting for the sake of experiment and experiment for the sake of art—as Martha Graham, and George Balanchine, and Herbert Migdoll do.   —WALTER SORELL

Migdoll photographed most of the dancers shown in the preceding portfolio in New York City, which today is considered the dance center of the world both for the quality and the quantity of the work performed.

1 Outfitted in costumes that hide human contours, their expressionless faces whitened with make-up, the stick figures in Alwin Nikolais's Imago are thoroughly depersonalized. Transformed into abstract objects, they move to the sound of electronic music.

2 Martha Graham's The Witch of Endor is drawn from Samuel, Book I, of the Old Testament, in which Saul seeks out a soothsayer (the witch, played by Miss Graham, is shown in the photograph).

The witch leads Saul to a vision of Samuel, revealed with bone-chilling suddenness in the abstract "gate" designed by Ming Cho Lee. A perfect marriage of classical theme and modern interpretation, the dance is vintage Graham.

3 In George Balanchine's spirited Harlequinade Columbine is swept into the air by her lover, Harlequin. A reworking of a ballet originally done at St. Petersburg in 1900, Balanchine's story ballet is in the tradition of slapstick commedia dell' arte and features the stock comic characters Pierrot, Pierrette, and Scaramouche.

4 Carolee Schneeman's dance happening Water Light/Water Needle was originally done indoors at St. Mark's

Church in the Bouwerie. Critics called it "an almighty bore," but performed later in a splashing vernal version outside the city, it seemed good sport.

5 The Polish Mime Theatre's Labyrinth begins with a clash of cymbals and is then performed in silence. "Now and then a lone figure would yearn forward," according to one critic. "Like a Kokoschka figure, he seemed in pursuit of freedom which constantly eluded him."

6 The suave moves of a bullfighter are incorporated in one of a series of dances about the life cycle of the Tarascan Indians, performed by the Ballet Folklórico de Mexico. Subsidized by the Mexican government, the company has come to America regularly since 1958.

By J. H. PLUMB

THE ANARCHY OF ART

Wandering through the galleries of London, New York, or Paris is a bewildering experience for a liberal-minded man of fifty. After all, in our youth we had our moments of excitement and protest. We were seized by bitter fury against the Establishment when the police seized D. H. Lawrence's etiolated nudes. And how we laughed at the glossy horrors of Munnings —those beautiful scrubbed gypsies, the scented winds blowing through their tresses; and the horses—oh, the horses! So worthy of a royal behind. And what derision we felt for the heavy, momentous portraits of tycoons that littered the board rooms of London and New York.

We thronged to the surrealists—disturbed, perhaps, by the weird landscapes of Tanguy, seemingly full of colored, floating contraceptives; worried somewhat by Dali's soft watches, by Ernst's terrifying forests, and by Magritte's meticulously painted shocks. But we had read our Freud and we knew the language of dreams, so we could participate in the pictures without great difficulty. Nor did Picasso's distorted females or the abstractions of Nicholson trouble us overmuch, any more than the new sculpture of Brancusi, Archipenko, or Moore. The persuasive effects of scientific ideas made even the most abstract works seem relevant; that pure form and pure mathematics might have a resonance seemed possible to the untutored humanist. And the traditional art that we knew had always possessed both geometric and algebraic qualities. And so one could reach through to Jackson Pollock—painting without language but decorative, memorable, at times haunting. With abstraction, however, one was getting near the boundaries of contact, feeling not only a lack of intuition but also a deadness, as if chords were being hammered on a dumb piano.

But now, how does one find one's way through the present anarchy of art, which ranges so wildly from the meticulous studies of Wyeth to the cold remains of the postwar surrealism of Moore, to the near-abstractions of Sutherland, to the screaming, bleeding faces of Francis Bacon, to the cartoon horrors of Pop, to Bridget Riley's literally painful Op, or to the junk and graffiti schools, the hard-edge types, or those anti-art artists who just paint shapeless boards one color and leave them lying on the floor or propped up against a wall? Must one turn one's back on all this, denounce it as infantile, regressive, anarchic, or mad—neither decorative nor meaningful? Has art, after living within one broad context for centuries, shattered into fragments? Is there anywhere to go?

Of course, there has always been a mad fringe in art, an exhibitionistic desire to shock, to blitz the viewer out of his compliant acceptance of the reality that he sees. After all, Bosch did not paint to soothe but to terrify, to hammer home the evil in men's nature and its terrible consequences; this is no different, perhaps, from Francis Bacon, no matter how far apart the two may be in technique or subject. Even Pop Art has a long history behind it, going back really as far as Daumier, Doré, Hogarth, and beyond. Few abstract impressionists have been as good as Turner, even though he called his compositions steam and sky. Some artists have always wanted to give us new eyes, to make us learn a new language of the heart; others—and these usually have been the major artists—have accepted the artistic conventions of their day, have bent and exploited them to the limits of their ingenuity and need but kept always just within the context of the language of art of their time. Leonardo, Michelangelo, Velasquez, Rembrandt, Chardin, Goya are firmly embedded in the artistic tradition of their age, no matter how adventurous they might be in technique or subject matter.

Indeed, about most great ages of art there is a harmony between painting, sculpture, music, architecture, and the decorative arts that is unmistakable and clear. That the music of Handel should be heard in the Assembly Rooms at Bath, which were adorned by the pictures of Gainsborough and embellished with the furniture of Chippendale, seems as natural as the powdered hair, the satin clothes, the enameled snuffboxes, and the teacups of Chelsea china. They are as harmonious as notes in music, as harmonious as the golden stone of the city that blends with the Cotswold Hills. That we ourselves endow such a scene with some measure of unity and harmony I do not doubt, but try as one might it is impossible to unite the elegance of the Seagram Building with the painted beds of Rauschenberg or the cacophonic horrors of *musique concrète.* In the eighteenth century this overriding unity of taste was established and maintained by a small coterie of well-informed connoisseurs who could insist on their standards because they were the sole patrons. And even if this made for some conservatism, against which, to our loss, a Mozart might chafe, it also provided a welcome balance against ignorance, vulgarity, and a heedless search for novelty.

There can be no doubt that the growth of the middle class led to diversity and insecurity in artistic taste and production. Bouguereau on the one hand and Manet

on the other are indicative of the onset of schizophrenia—and, worse still, of the onset of a much more intense commercialization of art than any previous century had known. The avant-garde proved as exploitable as the academicians; and so by our own time did infants, grandmas, and chimpanzees.

The growth, therefore, of a large market for art helped to break the imposition of taste by the patron-connoisseur, but that is only part of the reason for the present anarchy. Looking back on the Renaissance, it seems a miracle that genius blossomed so freely in Florence, Venice, Rome, Milan, Perugia, Bergamo, Bologna, and a score of lesser towns. Where did they come from, these supreme artists—Masaccio, Piero della Francesca, Botticelli, Leonardo, Lippi, Cosimo, Michelangelo, Raphael. Unlike most miracles, this one repeated itself; for the cities of Holland and Flanders suddenly produced a crop of almost equally magnificent painters in the seventeenth century—Rubens, Hals, Van Dyck, Rembrandt, Cuyp, Vermeer—and the phenomenon was repeated yet again in the middle decades of the nineteenth century in France. Between these great periods, painters of astonishing invention and skill littered Europe with pictures sufficient to fill first its own museums, palaces, and noble houses and then those of America. Great painters are easier to come by than great poets or great musicians, or so it would seem.

Given the basic skills, painting is not a difficult art, and the number of human beings who can reach high technical accomplishment is probably very great. No other explanation can make sense. The graffiti scribblers, the junk artists, the abstractionists, and the rest have the techniques at their command. They can draw, compose; many have a wonderful sense of color. Rauschenberg's illustrations of Dante's *Inferno* make that point explicit enough. So the answer does not lie in the suggestion that other ages were more heavily endowed with geniuses than our own. Indeed the reverse is likely to be true. We probably have many more technically accomplished painters and sculptors than any previous age.

One factor is time: each age makes it more difficult for the next. It was much easier to be Aristotle in fourth-century-B.C. Athens than it is in twentieth-century New York; easier to be Newton in seventeenth-century Cambridge than in twentieth-century Moscow. Creative achievements of the highest order tend to open a wonderful field for secondary talent to exploit and cultivate but tend to limit the areas for supreme genius. The Renaissance painters created a magic-lantern world of perspective in which the viewer and artist could participate, but it was a world of myriad possibilities that took more than four centuries for artists of the most diverse natures and talents to really exploit. But with impressionism its resources had been well-nigh exhausted and pressure for technical ingenuity grew.

And there is a further, more profound difficulty: originality is just as rare in painters and sculptors as in engineers or chess players. Yet the development of the past hundred years of art has been the creation of a cult of the artist as a wayward, misunderstood, yet dedicated genius—the man exiled from society by the originality of his ideas and techniques. Hence the endless pursuit of novelty in modern art. Much of its so-called originality, however, is flat-footed, dull, obvious, jejune. Of course one can see immediately the point of Claes Oldenburg's simulated ironing boards, or sagging three-way plugs, or those man-size hamburgers. Criticism of our modern, supermarket, consumer society is better done in an essay. It is much, much more powerfully argued by a Galbraith or a Packard. And so the hamburgers do not shock, they just bore. The same is true of a great deal of Pop Art. Of course one can see the point of a meticulously painted Stars and Stripes in a frame; the trouble is that one can see it in a split second, and so the picture is as dead as a dodo before it begins. This kind of modern art is just as banal, just as empty of content, as the most tedious forms of salon painting.

Many artists, once they are driven to be original, are lost. They need to work in strong pictorial conventions, where technical virtuosity is at a premium, or better still in the wake of a major technical release such as the exploration of perspective, or landscape, or the nude, or even impressionism or surrealism, where the elements of the language are given. But to expect great painters to be original both in content and technique is rather like asking a novelist or poet to invent a language before he writes in it.

To dismiss all modern art as worthless is folly. Color and shape have always possessed beauty for the human eye, and much modern art is wondrous in color, as decorative as any that the world has given birth to. But decoration is not enough. Human beings must return as subjects of art. There is a need to return, above all, to the most haunting of all subjects—the human face. This surely is the artist's infinity, which neither imagination, technique, passion, nor wisdom can ever exhaust. And its rarity is for me one of the more depressing features of modern art.

Meanwhile, where do we middle-aged liberals go? Where can we look in order to praise? It is impossible to return to the academics. It seems rather staid to stop dead with Picasso or the surrealists, yet we are too old to be bored to death by the Rauschenbergs, Oldenburgs, Klines, and Cohens: too old for childish eroticism or flat-footed social comment. So one wanders, as along a seashore littered with debris; occasionally there are bits and pieces that delight the eye, more rarely a fragment of treasure, but the skies are gray, the wind coming in from the sea, very cold. There is nowhere to go but Coney Island.

Never mind discovering the origin of the universe,
just hanging around the telescope for a night
at Mount Palomar is a pleasant way to pass some relative time

A NIGHT AT THE OBSERVATORY

By HENRY S. F. COOPER, JR.

A year ago last summer, I was invited out to Mount Palomar, the big observatory in southern California, to spend a night on the two-hundred-inch telescope. A member of the observatory's staff wrote me exuberantly, "The scientists here feel that the last couple of years have been the most exciting in astronomy since Galileo." He was referring to observations of the quasars, most of which had been made at Mount Palomar. Quasars are thought to be tremendously distant objects that may be almost as old as the universe itself; as yet, not a great deal is known about them. "Dr. Jesse L. Greenstein, Executive Officer of the Department of Astronomy at Cal Tech, will be going down to Palomar soon, and he says he will be glad to have you go along," my correspondent continued. "He says to warn you not to expect any great discoveries." That was an acceptable condition. As a final admonition, he added that the telescope is extremely delicate, and before I went out I had to promise to do my best not to break it. This, I thought, would be an easy promise to keep, since the telescope is as big as a small freighter.

On my way to Palomar, I stopped in Pasadena at the California Institute of Technology, which runs the observatory. A smog that made one's eyes smart hung over the city. I found that Dr. Greenstein was already at Palomar, a hundred and thirty-five miles to the south and fifty-six hundred feet up in the clearer, cooler air. I headed south, too. The road wound through ranches and forest up and up a mountain. Soon I saw across a valley, perched on the edge of a plateau, the glistening aluminum dome of the observatory. The huge slit for the telescope to peer through was shut like a closed eyelid.

On top of the plateau, which was

The huge Hale telescope, seen from the floor of the Palomar observatory in the "fish-eye" photograph opposite, is the largest reflecting telescope in the world. Its 200-inch mirror is at lower left; at right, silhouetted by a patch of sky, is the elevator to the prime-focus cage.

dotted with nine sturdy yellow cottages, I headed toward the Monastery, where I expected to find Dr. Greenstein. The Monastery is the dormitory where the astronomers stay when they are using the two-hundred-inch telescope or the smaller forty-eight-inch Schmidt telescope. The Monastery is a solid building fitted out with black leather blinds for daytime sleeping. It was six o'clock in the evening. Dr. Greenstein, who had been up all the night before, was in the dining room having a solitary supper; a stocky, graying man in his mid-fifties who sported a tiny, pencil-thin moustache, he was the only astronomer on the mountain. Dr. Greenstein complained about not being able to sleep. "The first night I'm down here, I can't sleep at all," he said. "It isn't until the fifth day that I get a full night's, or rather morning's, sleep, and then it's time to go back to Pasadena." I asked him how often he had to go through this sleepless state, and he answered that in his case it was about thirty-five nights a year.

"I get up here whenever I can," he went on, planting an elbow next to a half-empty coffee cup. "Time on the telescope is so valuable that you snatch at it whenever you can get it. Just *having* the two-hundred-inch telescope puts Cal Tech in a tough spot. It's a national asset, so we can't do anything trivial. Any reasonably good astronomer would have to try hard in order *not* to make an interesting discovery with it. In practice it is used mainly by the members of the Department of Astronomy, and even with just sixteen of us, we are forever feuding to get time on the telescope. Cloudy time can be a real disaster."

I said I hoped Dr. Greenstein wouldn't be clouded out tonight, and he replied that he didn't think he would be. Since he had some preparations to make for the evening's work, I accompanied him along a path from the Monastery through a dry, prickly field toward the dome. It was partially hidden over the brow of a hill; for all any-

one could tell, a big silver balloon had crash-landed there.

I asked Dr. Greenstein whether he had been involved with quasars lately. He shrugged. "I feel that my work, which is mostly the composition of stars within our galaxy, is more important; and current interpretations of quasars may be obsolete by next week." Although Dr. Greenstein is best known for his studies of the evolution of stars and galaxies, and of the elements within the stars, he is a top quasar man, too, and he has made observations to learn what their composition might be.

Quasars were first noticed in 1960 by radio astronomers as invisible sources of radio waves. One of these sources, 3C-48, was identified with what appeared to be a tiny, sixteenth-magnitude star. Three years later Dr. Maarten Schmidt, at Palomar, managed to concentrate on film enough of the feeble light from a quasar to get a spectrum. It appeared that quasars were not tiny stars within our own galaxy, as had been thought, but instead probably were intense and incredibly distant sources of light and radio waves. Quasar 3C-48 appears to be almost four billion light-years away, and subsequently other quasars have been measured out to almost nine billion light-years away; this is four-fifths of the way back to the "big bang" with which the universe supposedly began.

By studying the quasars, it may be possible to learn whether the universe will expand indefinitely; or whether it will stop some day; or whether it will fall back in upon itself for another big bang—and if so, when these events will take place. But a great deal more information is needed about the quasars, including the answer to why they shine so much more brightly than even the brightest galaxies. This is a problem that Dr. Greenstein is working on.

"As it happens, I don't like working with quasars," Dr. Greenstein continued as we trudged along. "They're tricky little things. I don't even like the word 'quasar.' It was invented by a Chinese astronomer in New York

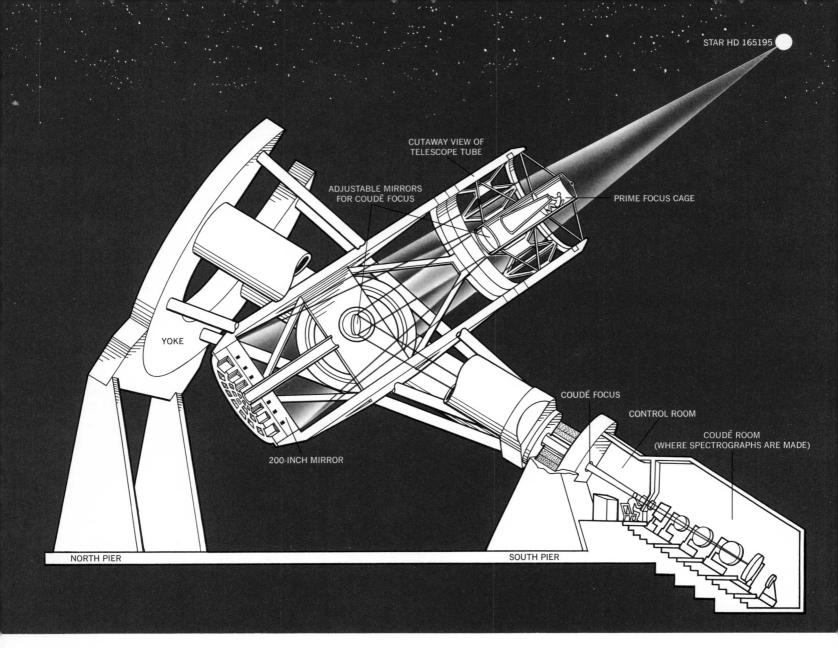

STAR HD 165195

CUTAWAY VIEW OF
TELESCOPE TUBE

ADJUSTABLE MIRRORS
FOR COUDÉ FOCUS

PRIME FOCUS CAGE

YOKE

COUDÉ FOCUS

CONTROL ROOM

COUDÉ ROOM
(WHERE SPECTROGRAPHS ARE MADE)

200-INCH MIRROR

NORTH PIER

SOUTH PIER

who doesn't speak English well. Chinese is like Hebrew, which has no vowels. He saw the letters QSRS, which stand for quasi-stellar radio source, on a chart, and called them 'quasars.' We shouldn't have a vocabulary for what we don't know, and when we do know what the quasars are, we will have a better word for them. Quasar sounds as if it's short for quasi-star, and that's the one thing we know a quasar isn't.'' Dr. Greenstein observed that the sky, darkening fast now, was beautifully clear. The moon, about half full, was rising in the east, clear crystal against the dark blue background, which, Dr. Greenstein said, augured well for seeing tonight. The setting sun glinted red on the dome. Dr. Greenstein glanced at

the cirrus clouds in the west, which were reddening as the sun sank. "Sunsets are nice," he said, "but you haven't seen anything until you see a sunrise at Palomar.''

The dome, which is nine stories tall and as much as that in diameter, rises from a round, yellow, cement drum. Dr. Greenstein fitted a key in a latch, and soon we were blinking our eyes inside a cavernous, pitch-black room three stories below the telescope. Dr. Greenstein said he had some work to do in his darkroom and suggested I go to the third floor and take a look at the telescope.

The inside of the dome was stuffy, dim, mysterious, and silent except for the echo of some approaching foot-

In operation the Hale telescope resembles nothing so much as a large bucket made to gather light. The mirror collects light and bounces it fifty-five feet up to a focal point where the prime-focus cage is located. For spectrographic analysis, the light is reflected back down and out to the room at lower right.

steps. The telescope loomed in the center of the room, shadowy and intricate, its works mostly exposed, like a fine timepiece under a glass bell. The telescope, Dr. Greenstein had told me, works something like a clock. Its tube has to keep time exactly with the movement of the stars so that a star's light can stay riveted to a photographic plate for several hours at a stretch. The telescope, with its reflecting mirror two hundred inches in diameter, serves as a sort of bucket to catch as much light as possible from a star and concentrate it on film: it could pick up the light of a ten-watt bulb a million miles away. The purpose of the telescope is not to magnify, for no matter how great the magnification, no star would ever show up as more than a point of light.

The footsteps I had heard belonged to the night assistant for the telescope, Gary Tuton, a lean young man with short, wavy hair. Tuton is the technician who runs the telescope for the astronomers. He walked over to a control console and pressed a button. The telescope sprang into life. The big mirror, which weighs almost fifteen tons, rests at the bottom of the telescope tube, an open steel cylinde some sixty feet long. The tube swivels north and south inside a huge frame called the yoke, and the yoke swivels from east to west on two enormous bearings, so that the tube, with the mirror at its bottom, can aim at any point in the sky.

Now the yoke spun to the east and the tube swiveled to the north, only, since both these motions happened simultaneously, the movement was one smooth undulation. The tube can be locked on a star, just as the pencil in a compass can be locked at any given radius. Then the star can be tracked along its path simply by turning the yoke, which is fixed on the North Star as if it were the dot at the center of a circle. The movement of the yoke has to be very delicate. Tuton explained that the huge bearings at either end of the yoke are floated on thin films of oil so that the telescope, which weighs five hundred tons, can be turned by hand. The oil pumps under the enormous bearings whined. The observatory sounded like a very active railroad yard.

Slowly and ponderously the two-hundred-and-twenty-five-ton doors that covered the slit in the dome pulled aside, revealing a widening band of dark blue sky. It was like being inside the eye of an awakening animal. "Sometimes, in winter, when the dome is cov-

ered with snow, I have to go up top and sweep the snow off the slit," Tuton said. "One night last winter it got so cold that the gears on the doors that cover the slit in the dome froze. No matter what I did, one shutter would shut and the other wouldn't, and there was a snowstorm coming. But by and large the weather is pretty good up here. Last year we used the telescope on three hundred and ten nights."

A door banged and Dr. Greenstein appeared, struggling under a load of lenses and photographic film. Since it was still too early to begin taking pictures, Dr. Greenstein said that he was going up into the prime-focus cage at the top of the telescope tube and invited me to come along. "I want to take a look at a group of stars, a globular cluster called Messier 13," he said. "There's a peculiar star in it that I want to get a spectrum of later on. It's in with such a mass of other stars that I want to make sure I get my bearings straight."

Dr. Greenstein explained that the prime focus was the simplest and most direct way of looking through the telescope. There are several different ways, and none of them is the conventional one, used with binoculars or refractor telescopes, of holding the telescope up to your eyes. Instead of focusing light through a lens, the big mirror bounces the light back up the tube and concentrates it at a point fifty-five feet above. The exact spot is called the prime focus. The astronomer sits in the prime-focus cage, which is like a balloonist's basket high inside the telescope tube, and from this vantage point he can photograph the image directly.

"I like it in the prime-focus cage," Dr. Greenstein concluded. "You feel closer to the stars." Then he frisked himself and me, removing any hard objects, such as coins and pens, that might fall on the mirror and damage it. It had taken eleven years to polish the mirror into exactly the right configuration; a scratch could mean years more polishing. We climbed to a balcony, boarded the dome elevator, and began a long,

hair-raising ascent as the elevator rose upward and outward, following the overhanging contour of the dome. Through the slit we could see the ground several stories below, and several thousand feet below that, the lights of the valley floor. The dome elevator is a peculiar, unenclosed contraption like a long spoon; we stood at the outer end of it where the bowl would be. After a bumpy ride, the elevator deposits the astronomer, like a dollop of medicine, inside the mouth of the telescope. At this point, the astronomer is about seventy feet above the floor of the dome, with very little to hang on to.

"People have gotten killed on telescopes," Dr. Greenstein said with what I thought was poor timing as we lurched unevenly up and out. "Sometimes astronomers get squashed by a telescope slewing about, but that doesn't happen very often."

I gripped the railing of the elevator, fixed my eyes firmly on the top of the dome, and asked Dr. Greenstein to tell me more about the peculiar star in Messier 13. "Globular clusters, like Messier 13, are sort of suburbs of our galaxy which contain some of the oldest stars, and for this reason they might have a bearing on the quasars, which are supposed to be primordial objects, too," he said. "However, the star I want to look at now is blue, a color usually associated with younger stars, so in this case it must represent a peculiar stage of evolution. Although this star—Barnard 29—is blue, it has a peculiar energy distribution. Its spectrum is too much in the red, and one possibility I want to check tonight is whether it couldn't in fact be a close pair, a double star, one blue and one red."

Soon we were directly on top of the telescope tube, and Dr. Greenstein flung open a flimsy gate at the end of the elevator platform. The prime-focus cage—a bucket perhaps five feet in diameter and five feet deep—was about eighteen inches below us. Dr. Greenstein explained that the elevator couldn't go all the way to the cage because of

the danger of collision with the telescope: we would have to travel across the remaining gap ourselves. So saying, he flung himself into the void and disappeared into the mouth of the telescope.

Inside the bucket was a chair and an empty well that looked straight down at the mirror; the astronomer fits his instruments into the well. When Tuton was sure that we were safely installed, and that nothing could drop on the mirror, he opened the diaphragm that covered it. Slowly, like a water lily, the petals of the diaphragm lifted, revealing what looked like a pond of rippling, shimmering water beneath. The stars, which wouldn't stay still, were streaking like meteors; the mirror, it seemed, was popping a few millionths of an inch with the change of temperature. Tuton slewed the telescope off in search of Messier 13 and Barnard 29. As one side of the bucket dipped suddenly down, the chair, which was on rails, moved around and down with gravity, so that the astronomer was always upright; the sensation was like riding very slowly in a Ferris wheel. Stars shot through the big mirror as we sailed along. The telescope came to a smooth halt, moving just fast enough to keep the stars still in spite of the rotation of the earth. Dr. Greenstein peered into the pool of light for a moment. Then he maneuvered a tiny lens that looked like a magnifying glass—it was tied to the well with a string—until he found the exact spot where the image was clearest. This was the prime focus.

"We're right on the beam," Dr. Greenstein said, handing the lens to me. As I looked down, I felt my glasses begin to slide down my nose; I grabbed them just before they dropped down the well toward the mirror. The lens resolved the chaotic splotches of dancing light, and I saw an enormous rash of stars, each one a point of hard, brilliant light. I couldn't make out Bar-

Dwarfed by the telescope's huge frame, an astronomer stands on the mirror casing prior to its installation at the observatory in 1948.

nard 29. Dr. Greenstein was able to converse with Tuton over an intercom, and he asked him to stop the telescope's tracking drive. No sooner had the telescope stopped moving than Messier 13 and Barnard 29 slipped out of the field of vision. Other stars whizzed across the mirror, following Messier 13 into seeming oblivion; a given star crossed the mirror in about ten seconds, before vanishing. That, Dr. Greenstein said, showed how fast the earth, with the telescope, was turning. Tuton's voice crackled through the microphone, asking how I felt. I replied that I was getting a little dizzy. Tuton started up the tracking device; the telescope passed all the stars that had been whipping by, and soon we were safely back with Messier 13.

"Did Dr. Greenstein tell you about the time I was stuck up there?" Tuton asked; and his voice crackled on, "I was in the prime-focus cage when the power for the telescope shorted out. It was a cold winter night. I had to climb down, which was the hairiest thing I ever did. What made me do it was not the cold so much as what the men who came in the morning would say. I'd never have lived it down."

At last Tuton wafted the telescope toward the elevator platform for us to board. I fixed my eye on the top of the dome again. Dr. Greenstein glanced at his watch and said that he wished the elevator would hurry, because it was already dark enough to start using the spectrograph. He shouted down to Tuton to start setting up the telescope for the coudé focus. The coudé focus is in a room outside the telescope altogether, and the light from a star is deflected to it by a mirror—called the coudé flat—which bounces the starlight in a thin beam down through a hole in the southern foundation of the telescope and into the coudé room one floor below, where the spectrographs are kept. The film to record the spectrum of a star is in this room, which serves something of the purpose of an old Brownie box camera. As we reached

the ground, an electronic engine whirred and the coudé flat, weighing a ton and a half, lifted slowly into position just below the prime-focus cage. It glittered like a jewel inside a watch.

Dr. Greenstein fetched the films he had brought with him and disappeared down the steps into the coudé room, a tiny chamber that descends steeply in line with the yoke, pointing at the North Star. It was already after eight o'clock. Barnard 29 was nestled among so many stars that the final zeroing in had to be done by dead reckoning. "There's a sort of triangle of stars," said Dr. Greenstein, who had returned to the control room at the top of the steps. "See it? There ought to be a double star on the upper left. Got it?" He sounded like a man finding his way with a road map. Tuton said he had it. "Do you know what the most difficult object to find is?" Tuton asked as he turned a knob for fine adjustment; I said I didn't. "It's the moon. The moon is so close, and it's moving so fast, that it's like trying to aim a rifle at a moving target close by, instead of at the trees standing behind it."

All of a sudden, Barnard 29 disappeared from view. It was as if the telescope had gone dead. Tuton raced out into the dome and peered up at the sky through the slit; a long, wispy cloud was obstructing the view. "Looks like it's going to be a cloud-dodging night," he said. Quickly Tuton and Greenstein flipped the telescope to another star, called HD 165195, which was in a cloudless part of the sky.

I asked Dr. Greenstein whether we would see any quasars that night. "The moon is up, so we can't work on anything as dim as quasars," he said. "That's probably just as well. There isn't much you can tell by looking at a quasar anyway. Instead, I will be doing long exposures on some of the oldest stars in the galaxy. The procedure is much the same as with quasars; and in fact part of what we'll be doing is related to quasars. There is a theory that has to be explored that the quasars are a remnant of the first formation of galaxies. According to this theory, during the contraction of the gases that formed the galaxies, some super-massive objects formed within them. These objects may have become extremely dense and pulled themselves together so rapidly that they exploded. Perhaps that is what the quasars are. I don't know. I'm fairly neutral on the subject. There is evidence in our own galaxy of a superexplosion far greater than the explosion of a supernova, but less, I think, than a quasar explosion. In any event, if the quasars represent monumental explosions within galaxies during the half-billion years or so that the galaxies and the stars were condensing out of primeval gas clouds, then you would expect that the oldest stars, the first to condense from the gases, would be heavily contaminated by the elements in the quasars. They would have been loaded with the products of quasar evolution."

Dr. Greenstein turned out the lights in the control room and pressed a button to start the exposure. The control room was lit only by the soft-green glow of the dials on the control panel, like the cockpit of an airplane at night. "So I will be looking at some of the oldest stars in our galaxy, like this one, to see whether they have the same elements and in roughly the same proportions, as the quasars. We don't know yet the exact composition of the quasars, but we may be able to do something with oxygen or iron. If they have the same elements, it might indicate quasars were the raw material in forming stars. But if there are other elements aside from those found in quasars, it might prove that the quasars are not important in star evolution, for the oldest stars don't seem to have manufactured many new elements after their formation, such as metals. But if I find a trace of metal in HD 165195, I have to decide whether it might have been cooked within the star after all, or whether the metal was part of the original gases of which the star was composed. The chances are we won't know

much more after tonight. I'll need this type of information on hundreds of stars before I can begin to get anywhere."

The time was eight-thirty. I found myself standing in the path of the slender stream of light from HD 165195, and Dr. Greenstein asked me to step out of the way, which wasn't easy, since the control room was cramped and narrow. A ticking sound filled the room. Dr. Greenstein said that the ticking came from the photoelectric scaler, which counts the number of photons coming from a star, like a light meter. Each tick meant twenty thousand photons of light. A dial kept count of the ticks, and Dr. Greenstein said that, for this exposure, he wanted about thirty-three hundred.

He invited me to look through the eyepiece of the spectrograph. A spectrograph, an apparatus in the control room that intercepted the light coming from HD 165195, refracts and spreads out the light from a star into its component wave lights, giving a spectrum something like the light from a prism. The lines in a spectrum show the elements in a star. They also show how fast an object is receding from the earth by how much the lines are shifted to the red end of the spectrum. This is called the red shift, and it was in this way that Schmidt first decided the quasars were tremendously distant objects. Through the eyepiece, the star appeared as a fuzzy, bright-green spark; the star's light had been shattered by passing through a slit and some gratings inside the spectrograph. Dr. Greenstein said the light had left the star ten thousand years ago. Tuton darted across to the telescope's control panel and slowed down the telescope's tracking drive by a tiny fraction. "We want to make the star trail along the slit in the spectrograph," he said. "This is what we have to do with faint objects. It's like painting one brush stroke over another, until you get the proper intensity on the plate."

With everything squared away, Tu-

ton settled down by the eyepiece, stretched, yawned, and tuned in a radio to a rock-'n'-roll station in San Bernardino. He kept an ear cocked to make sure the ticking didn't stop, and every once in a while he checked the eyepiece to make sure the star was still there. I asked Dr. Greenstein why he and the other astronomers couldn't stay in Pasadena, and phone down to Tuton whenever they wanted a plate taken of a star. "There are too many things that can go wrong," Dr. Greenstein said. "I wouldn't know whether a plate was any good or not unless I was here." Tuton concurred with him. "I've never been trained in astronomy," he said. "I can run the telescope all right, and find a star, but when it comes to astronomy, I just haven't the foggiest idea what's going on. The astronomer never says what he's doing. Half the time he doesn't know what he's done until he's gotten back to Pasadena. I didn't know anything about quasars until I read about them in the papers." Then Tuton pulled out a magazine, which he squinted at by the light of the dials.

Dr. Greenstein suggested that we go out on the catwalk. Except for a gentle breeze, the plateau was absolutely still. I could see the smaller dome of the Schmidt telescope about half a mile to the east. Dr. Greenstein pointed out a spot between the two domes where an Air Force bomber had crashed four years earlier, killing the crew and two horses that belonged to the superintendent of the observatory but miraculously doing no damage to the telescope. Away to the northwest, the smog over Los Angeles glowed—possibly in something of the way the outer gases of the quasars shine, powered by some mysterious force inside. There was a light mist on the mountain, and the half-moon glowed overhead. "Only spectrograph work can be done in full moonlight, and even that is terribly difficult," Dr. Greenstein said. "You have to be very careful that the moonlight doesn't contaminate your plate. I thought I'd made a great spectro-

graphic discovery once, only to find that it was the light of the moon, and not of the star. There is a gadget called a moon eliminator. I wish we could get rid of the moon for good!''

Dr. Greenstein glanced at his watch. It was eleven o'clock. "The night's young yet," he said energetically. He went inside, bustled into the control room, checked the dial that counted the ticks, and shut down the spectrograph. Tuton slewed the telescope to another star, BD 39°4926, which Dr. Greenstein explained was also very old and might shed light on whether quasars had to do with galaxy formation. Then, since the exposure would last for three hours, Dr. Greenstein went

downstairs to his darkroom to develop the plate on HD 165195.

Amid a sloshing of water and the acrid odor of hypo Dr. Greenstein said, "I don't really believe that the older stars are residues of quasars. I don't believe the quasars are a part of galaxies, and therefore I don't happen to believe that they have anything to do with star evolution. There is evidence of giant explosions in galaxies now, but whether these caused quasars or not, we don't know. But what we know of quasars really isn't conducive to the formation of stars. I don't believe quasars come from explosions, though other astronomers do. Speculation is like the stock market. I feel that the quasars instead may be in

some kind of balance condition, like a star, and that they are isolated objects, and that they are formed of matter between galaxies. Other people feel they are little things which have been blown out of galaxies. Another group believes that the quasars are extremely dense objects and that their red shifts are caused by gravity, rather than by speed or distance. I don't know. The best we can do is to test the different theories, which is what I'm trying to do now."

Just after midnight, Dr. Greenstein came up from the darkroom. He checked the star, which was ticking away nicely on the slit, and sat on a table. "That's all the developing I do tonight," he said. "It's too risky when you're tired." He had evidently lost his second wind. I asked him if he had been able to tell anything about HD 165195, and he said he hadn't. "It's too late at night for discoveries," he said with a yawn. "There's nothing like making a great discovery that you might absent-mindedly wipe off the plate with a wet finger. I make it a rule never to make great discoveries after midnight."

Dr. Greenstein yawned again. I followed him over to a couple of reclining chairs by the control console under the north bearing. Just visible in the starlight, he lay back with his arms folded behind his head as a pillow and his eyes shut. The moon, for the time being, was obscured, so it was unusually dark inside the dome. As I became more accustomed to the darkness—it was much darker than in the control room, which contained a number of luminous dials—I could make out more and more of the telescope. Dr. Greenstein opened his eyes. "I could look at it forever," he said. "No matter how long you look at it, it always looks different. It looks different now, when you can barely see it in the dim starlight, from what it did a few minutes ago in the light of the half-moon. It's different from whatever side you look at it. Right now, it just sits there and broods. It is a remarkable subordination of brute force for delicate ends. All this mechanism is for is to move one piece of glass; and all the glass is for is to carry one thin layer of aluminum that reflects starlight. I wish it were quieter! We must get rid of those oil pumps."

At last Dr. Greenstein's voice drifted off. He was fast asleep. After a time he sat bolt upright and looked at his watch. It was two fifteen. Above him, the telescope was almost completely on its side, as if it, too, had been asleep. Over the last three hours, its tracking of BD 39°4926 had caused it to as-
sume this position. The ticking ceased abruptly when Dr. Greenstein checked the meter and ended the exposure. After rummaging around in the inky coudé room to change plates, Dr. Greenstein came back to the control room and decided to return to Barnard 29. "We need about three hours, though with this much moon, I doubt if we'll get it," he said briskly as he zeroed in the telescope. As he was talking, the ticking became more and more sporadic, slowing down; finally it stopped altogether. Tuton, who had had no nap, and who looked a little scruffy, went out under the dome and squinted up through the slit. Barnard 29 was obscured by clouds again. "What do we do now?" Tuton asked Greenstein. Tuton said that what he would like to do now would be go home and go to bed.

"We're getting only about ten minutes' exposure time to the hour, but as long as I can get even that much, I can't shut down," Dr. Greenstein said, and added unhappily, "the telescope's time is more valuable than my own." It costs one thousand dollars a night to operate the telescope. Suddenly a great rift appeared in the clouds, and the moon emerged. It was greeted with a terrific burst of ticks. Dr. Greenstein shouted to Tuton to shut off the spectrograph. "We're better off wasting exposure time and not getting contamination," Dr. Greenstein grumbled, exhaling a cloud of cigar smoke that glowed derisively in the moonlight. It was a little after two forty-five, and I had the impression that Dr. Greenstein was about to call it a night.

At three fifteen the sky cleared and Tuton started the exposure once more. Since he was stiff and tired, Dr. Greenstein suggested another spin around the catwalk. There was low-lying mist on the plateau, and not far away a jay woke up raucously. The air was chill and damp. The east was as dark as ever, but Dr. Greenstein said he could see the zodiacal light, which heralds the dawn. "We won't be able to keep the exposure going much longer," he
went on. "The sun is already beginning to heat up the atmosphere to the east, which makes it bubble a bit." Groggily, I looked for bubbles in the east, but saw none. A flush of pink appeared and spread rapidly; the stars to the east blinked out, though the ones to the west were, for the time being, as hard and brilliant as they had been for most of the night. Shadows grew where none had been before, and we could begin to see colors—the green of the pines, the pink clay of the road. Dr. Greenstein went back inside and called down to Tuton to turn off the exposure before it was contaminated.

The inside of the dome was suffused with pink; the dome's interior, too, was of brilliant aluminum, and caught the dawn through the slit. The telescope was visible again, like a dinosaur emerging from a misty bog. "This is *my* time on the telescope," Tuton said, "the time after dawn, but before all the stars are washed out. It's useless for spectrography or photography, so I just aim the telescope at what I want to look at. I think Saturn is in a good position for viewing."

He consulted an astronomy book and quickly swung the telescope to a new position. He snapped the eyepiece into place, focusing it. He stepped aside, and I took a look. There was Saturn, as big as a football and, with its rings forming an oval around it, somewhat the same shape. Through the two-hundred-inch telescope, Saturn was so brilliant that it hurt the eyes. Dr. Greenstein squinted through the eyepiece, grunting. "I never particularly liked the solar system," he said, relinquishing the telescope. I looked again; Saturn was less brilliant than before, and it was fading fast in the sunlight. Soon it vanished altogether, like the Cheshire cat, leaving nothing behind but a patch of pale-blue sky.

Henry S. F. Cooper, Jr., a member of the editorial staff of The New Yorker, *writes frequently on scientific subjects.*

Turn the pages of the smallest Chinese-English vocabulary I know, and you will find useful everyday words and phrases like these:

hoo: to find bail for the lighter offences of females.

ch'he: devoid of intelligence, deficient of wit, silly, idiotic. Also used for borrowing and returning books.

maou tsaou: a scholar not succeeding and giving himself over to liquor.

Experts—differing as usual—assure us either that man makes his language or the language makes the man. These extracts from *The Chinese Unicorn*, which is based on a mid-nineteenth-century Chinese-English dictionary, therefore open a fanlight on Chinese society through which we can glimpse its curiosities (in this situation a Western inquirer begins to feel like a *pa*—defined as "a short man standing as high as he can").

On closer examination, we find more puzzling entries in the *Unicorn:*

wan: a small mouth. Some say a large mouth.

chen: to stand still. To gallop at full speed.

You dismiss these contradictions as the bet-hedging of an English missionary working on a little-known tongue more than a century before Suzie Wong, and consult a modern Chinese-English dictionary for the correct meanings—only to find something like this:

E: (in the *Unicorn*)—pig; some say a fox.

(in the modern dictionary)—"emulate," "strive after."

At this point even *heaou* ("a well-informed female mind") might feel as if her brain had gone a bit *sih* ("water dried up so as to make it difficult to sail a boat"), and pitch the *Unicorn* into the wastebasket. She might then with some sense of relief

look up a very simple or common Chinese character in the modern dictionary, with this result:

nai: then, now, so also, and, but, if, i.e., namely, accordingly, to be, your, theirs, his, her, its, that, those.

By now it will be realized that the Chinese written language may sometimes be a little imprecise. And this imprecision has been compounded from century to century almost as quickly as the Chinese have introduced new little complications in order to make their language clearer.

The ancestor of the modern Chinese character was the straightforward pre-Christian pictogram, like this one:

= *nu:* a woman.

The arm and leg positions, in particular, were supposed to indicate that this was a female: man was

(and is): 人 (or 亻).

But as writing became grace-

fully stylized, woman came to be written:

女

Pictograms were then combined with others to express more sophisticated if sometimes debatable ideas like:

安 (a woman under a roof) = peace.

好 (female with male child) = good.

and 姦 (three females) = adultery, fornication, debauch, ravish (some say a four-letter word).

The pictogram of a woman is one of 214 "radicals," at least one of which will form part of any Chinese character. The radicals are supposed to give some indication of the meaning of the character, much as "phil" at the beginning of a Romance word in English tells us that it is about love—but no more. A stranger to the word "philately" may

guess wildly at erotic connotations and be faintly astonished to find it means stamp collecting after all, and in Chinese the pits are dug even deeper. A character may have five component parts, including two or three possible radicals, but its meaning may have nothing to do with the radical, and its sound nothing to do with its phonetic element. Or it may be highly allusive:

如 = woman + mouth

originally meant "follow" (a woman obeys orders from the mouth). From "follow" it came to mean "like" (to follow, to be like), and from "like" it came to mean "if" (like supposing).

The basic character: 表 (*piao*) means "to display." Put the "man" radical on its left:

俵 (*piao*) and it means "to distribute." Put the "woman" radical there: 婊 (*piao*) and it means "prostitute." But in the old days radicals were not attached to all characters to make these fine shades of meaning obvious. Sad errors could therefore creep in. And did.

Ideograms are in turn combined into pairs or groups to express more complicated meanings or phrases, and this system of word building may on occasion produce interesting results when a Chinese is struggling with English. ("And now," says my wife, Ping, at the London Zoo, "now we go to see the—the—the pocket mouse."

"The *what?*"

"The *pocket* mouse. *You* know. Put-in-the-pocket, *that* kind mouse!" And she traces the two characters for "pocket" and "mouse" on her palm. I am still in the dark, until she adds: "That bigger-than-you jumping-around boxing mouse. In *ao-ta-li-ya.*" Light dawns, and we set off for the kangaroos.)

By DENNIS BLOODWORTH

But literary Chinese has been essentially a laconic affair, with one character sometimes standing for a spoken word of three syllables that could only be fully expressed by three characters. It is just as if we wrote "autocracy" as "auto" and left the reader to work out that we did not mean "automobile."

A university student must be familiar with some 8,000 Chinese characters (there are roughly 45,000 in all) and their complex system of association with one another, and he has no alphabet to guide him through a dictionary. An ordinary Chinese typewriter looks more like a printer's type-setting machine. It has 2,590 "keys," and blank settings into which slugs of the rarer characters, taken from a reserve of a further 3,432, can be fitted as they are needed. A telegram in Chinese characters must be enciphered into a number code, the numbers transmitted in Morse, and then the groups translated back into characters by the recipient.

Throughout history the Chinese written language has been difficult to learn, and it was estimated even in the 1930's that only three million newspapers were sold daily in all China, to be read by perhaps one man in every twenty-five. The Communists, in their successful drive for literacy, have tried to simplify things by reducing the number of characters to 3,000 (there were still 8,000 in common use in 1965), and by stripping down the more complicated ones so that they are easier to memorize and write; but this has introduced the further complication that there are now two written Chinese languages, for Formosan and Overseas Chinese have stuck to the original ideograms.

That suits Peking perfectly, for it means that the "literate" young peasant or worker who has been given a limited educa-tion in Communist China in new basic Chinese is largely shut off from the deviationist writings printed in the more complex characters of the past. He now enjoys the benefits of a closed-circuit Communist culture. The masses are back where they were when they relied on a literate elite to tell them what was what.

It has been said that Chinese is an essentially feminine language dealing in concrete forms, so that abstracts cannot be properly expressed. There is no word for "size" (the Chinese say "big-small"), no word for "weight" (they say "light-heavy"), no word for "-ness." The ideograms are like a series of pictures, absorbed passively by the eye, whereas Western alphabetical script draws the reader forward along rails of writing as a man is taken along by a closely reasoned logical argument. Chinese, therefore, is not a language of ideas or of rational debate, some say.

But this argument can be taken too far. Great fun can doubtless be had by translating Chinese literally. How amusing that "psychology" should be rendered by three characters that signify "mind-principle-study," that "sympathy" should be "together-feel," "aesthetics" "beauty-learning," and "inexhaustible" "use-not-finish"—until we realize that these quaint transmogrifications precisely reflect the true visage of the English words behind their Latin or Greek face-packs. There seems no real reason to believe that the Chinese cannot feel abstract ideas just as keenly as a second-year Oxford fine arts student plagued by psychosomatic fleas.

The trouble with Chinese is not indistinctness but ambiguity. It has virtually no plural, no active or passive voice, no definite article, no syntax worth mentioning. It is highly idiomatic and has about as much legal precision as can be found in the common expression "Long time no see."

Ambiguity may be doubly dangerous in the mouths of the literal-minded, but to the Chinese the letter is nevertheless all-important. For, as Chinese writing is a series of symbols and not a phonetic system, it has the inestimable advantage that it can be read and understood by people who pronounce the names of those symbols quite differently from one another wherever Chinese is spoken.

For the complications of Chinese are not limited to the loopholes in the written language. In Singapore alone six main Chinese dialects are spoken, and our *amah* (servant) in Singapore cannot even talk to the one next door except in badly mauled Malay, although they look almost alike, for Ah Fu talks Cantonese and Ah Sim talks Hokkien. Communist, Nationalist, and most Overseas Chinese schools are now teaching the rising generation Mandarin, the national language based on the Peking dialect, but Singapore's Chinatown is still a tower of babel laid out flat.

This is one reason why it is difficult to Romanize Chinese, for you cannot produce a phonetic script that will be easily understood by, say, an Englishman, a Frenchman, and a Hungarian, who must respectively read the same written word as "square," "*carré*," and "*négyszög*." Show them a drawing of a square, however, and they all recognize it at once. That is what the ideogram, or character, does for Cantonese, Hokkien, Mandarin, and Hakka speakers alike. Separate Romanized systems have therefore to be devised for separate dialects (especially when, for example, "*yi*" means "one" in Mandarin, but "two" in Cantonese).

Chinese is a tonal language, and it makes a difference whether you say "*ching*" with a flat, an upward, a swooping, or a diving inflection. This aid to understanding—requiring as it does a sharp ear and a nimble, musical tongue—is not the only one. But that does not make it any the less disconcerting that a Mandarin-speaker will pronounce the written phrase "forty-four dead stone lions" as *ssu shih ssu shih shih*.

Every unfortunate foreigner who has been hooked by the Chinese language has had the experience, while floundering through the shallows, of ordering soup and getting sugar, or salt and getting tobacco, for the words in Chinese sound the same.

The opportunities for punning in Chinese are, obviously, almost limitless, and the very first sentence of Lao-tze—"The Way that can be spoken is not the eternal Way"—is strongly suspect, for *Tao* is used to mean not only "Way" but also "Speak," so that the sentence might be rendered "The Way that can be the Way is not the eternal Way," or "The Speech that can be spoken is not the eternal Speech."

Punning leads the Chinese into a curious realm of self-delusion, superstition, and symbolism, in which one thing tends to be represented by another and therefore to have no reality of its own. The First Emperor is told that if he buries a myriad men in the foundations of the Great Wall, it will endure a myriad years, for their spirits will protect it. But he avoids a massacre by immuring a single "Mr. Myriad," a hapless creature unfortunate enough to be born with the name of Wan, which is the sound of the character that means "ten thousand."

The Chinese delight in their language with its "pleasures shallow sorrows deep" economy of idiom, and would rather be concisely ambiguous than long-windedly lucid. And nothing, to the Chinese, could be more deliciously enigmatic for the uninitiated than my wife's full given-name, for Ching Ping means "Apprehensive Ice." This is a drastic contraction of the tag in the *Book of Odes* that reads: "We should be apprehensive and careful/As if we were on the brink of a deep gulf/As if we were treading on thin ice" (literally, "Apprehensive Careful/As If Brink Deep Gulf/As If Tread Thin Ice").

All this shrink-think leads to situations in which a house is considered uninhabitable because its previous owner called it "Sunset Heights"—which implies that to occupy it is to pass one's peak. Too often the responses of Chinese are narrow and mechanical. For centuries they learned the classics by rote, parroted improving slogans, memorized words rather than remembered their wisdom.

When I was last in China, officials always prefaced their answers to questions with the same robot phrase until I found myself hearing it even in the rhythm of a railway car—"*Thanks* to the *leader*ship of *Chair*man *Mao* and the *Chinese Com*munist *Par-tee* . . ." No homily was complete without it.

Then there are the finger-counting exercises for easy memorization—the "Three-Anti" campaign of 1951 (anti-corruption, anti-waste, and anti-bureaucratism), the "Five-anti" movement against bribery, tax evasion, fraud, theft of public property, betrayal of national economic secrets; and in the army there are the "Four-good companies" and the "Five-good fighters," and so on.

The Chinese recoil from the messiness of our untidy reality into their own wonderland of the pat answer and the solution ingenious. Three men want to divide seventeen oranges so that one gets half of them, another gets a third, and the other gets

WHITE GEM CONCUBINE COLD LIKE ICE FROST

Chinese pictograms labor to express day-to-day events—as the title on page 117, which means "Shrink-Think," implies. The subtitle (translated in part above) is, in truth, a *non sequitur*. It is rendered literally as "relations liberal bear cat white gem concubine small sister cold like ice frost," and it was taken from a headline on a story concerning the transport of a panda from London to Moscow. The panda, it seems, was so disturbed by the journey that it would not even give its mate, An-An, a kiss —or so the Chinese newspaper reported. For an English-speaking person to unravel that headline, given in full in the table below, it is necessary to go through three stages:

PRONOUNCED	LITERALLY	TRANSLATED
lun	relations	London
tun	liberal	
hsiung	bear	panda
mao	cat	
chi	white gem	Chi-Chi
chi	concubine	
hsiao	small	
chieh	sister	
leng	cold	very
juo	like	cold
ping	ice	
shuang	frost	
fei	fly	Flies to
mo	not	
ssu	this	Moscow
k'o	grade	
p'ei	mate	but
chung	seed	won't
pu	not	mate
ch'eng	succeed	
pu	not	Won't
kei	give	give
an	peace	An-An
an	peace	
yi	one	even a
ch'in	affectionate	
hsiang	fragrant	kiss
tse	flavor	

Proper names are written phonetically. Thus London is represented by the characters for *lun* and *tun*—which also have meanings in their own right: "relations," "liberal." Similarly, Moscow is written *mo-ssu-k'o*, which happens to mean "not this grade." An-An had to make do with the character *an*, meaning "peace," written twice; but for Chi-Chi the changes are rung by using two different meanings of *chi* with different pictograms, "white gem" and "sing-song girl" (concubine). "Small sister" in the subtitle serves only an emotive and decorative purpose. *Mao* here is "cat," not to be confused with *mao* as in Mao Tsetung, whose name means literally "Hair Enrich-East."

one-ninth of them. How is it done? A small boy comes along with one orange, which he throws into the pile. There are now eighteen. The first man takes nine, the second six, the third two. That accounts for seventeen of the oranges, and the small boy then takes his own back. This is the reality that delights the Chinese—reality with a magic orange in the wings.

In this sense life to the Chinese is a game of chess, in which the gambit, the ruse, and the little stratagem are often ends in themselves. "Very Chinese story," commented Apprehensive Ice when we walked out of the cinema after seeing the film *The Bridge on the River Kwai*, in which a British colonel, taken prisoner by the Japanese, builds a bridge for them and even gives his life trying to save it, so obsessed by pride in his work that he had forgotten it will serve the wrong cause.

There is no common denominator, no generic term, which can embrace all the loosely linked manifestations of this slightly gimicky quality in the Chinese mind that is so at odds with flexible, naturalistic Taoist teaching, this preference for the truth in the clock rather than the time itself. From punning to poetic justice, however, they have one thing in common: they confuse by seeming to clarify, for the more we try to tidy nature up, the more we obscure it. They are, in their neat suburban fashion, the enemies of the windy and shapeless open spaces of free inquiry, in which truths can sometimes be found, if not truth itself.

Dennis Bloodworth, Southeast Asia correspondent for The Observer, *lives in Singapore with his Chinese wife, Ching Ping. This article is taken from* The Chinese Looking-Glass, *which is being published this summer by Farrar, Straus & Giroux, Inc.*

QUENCHLESS ME AND OMPHALOCENTRIC YOU

In its quenchless vitality [the middle-aged generation] drinks up the golden decades like nectar at the banquet table of life. It is invisible because it defies chronology. It measures age not by a date on a calendar but by a dance of the mind.

Those were the words that I had been waiting for. Well, not *those* words exactly, but the idea that they were straining to express. In the youth-crazed journalism of modern America, awash with articles about all those finky kids under twenty-five who will soon outnumber the rest of us and who really run the country, here was a magazine that came right out and said something good for those of us who have turned forty. And that's not all it said.

[The middle-ager] can place Archimedes' lever in the exact spot that will shift the world a trifle closer to his heart's desire. . . . Before 40, one adds and feeds to gorge the ego; after 40, one subtracts and simplifies to slim the soul. . . . The young want to dynamite the treasure vaults of life; middle age has learned the combination.

I mean that's living, isn't it? Those kids think *they're* turned on? Man, we've got Archimedes' lever. They think *they've* found the nitty-gritty of life with their acid-head truths? Baby, we're inside the treasure vaults slimming the soul.

Or, rather, we were. We seem to be out again now. A mere five months after we learned the combination, it was snatched away by the same magazine. I need hardly identify the magazine as *Time*—nowhere but in a *Time* cover story do turgid generalities flower quite so richly. Besides, everyone between forty and sixty will remember the particular cover story from which I have taken these excerpts. Using Lauren Bacall as its symbol ("It is this mercury of the spirit, this added luster of vitality that adorns the beauty within the beauty of Lauren Bacall"), *Time* flatly declared us to be the "Command Generation": the "top-responsibility" men and women "who occupy the seats of power" and decide how the rest of America will live.

That was last summer—July 29, 1966— and I still remember what a tonic the article was. Command Generation! Us! For weeks afterward we carried our heads a little higher, our stomachs a little flatter. We

knew again what we had secretly begun to doubt: that we still *could* swim to the second float, ride that Honda, impress those mini-shifted nymphets on the beach with a lively dance of the mind. Oh, we were grateful to *Time* in those gilded months.

Of course I knew it couldn't last. Soon enough the winter frosts would chill the endocrine glands of middle-aged magazine editors and tilt the balance back to youth. But I didn't dream that it would happen so quickly, and so decisively, and in the same rococo prose. In fact, I had been expecting *Time*'s Man of the Year to be U Thant, or at the very least some scientist who had harnessed the laser beam or transplanted the vital organs of a rhesus monkey.

But who did it turn out to be? That finky kid! Man of the Year, right on the cover:

CHARMATZ

January 6, 1967. I hurried to the story inside to see what he had that we Command Generation folks suddenly didn't have.

With his skeptical yet humanistic outlook, his disdain for fanaticism and his scorn for the spurious, the Man of the Year suggests that he will infuse the future with a new sense of morality, a transcendent and contemporary ethic that could infinitely enrich the "empty society."

Well, obviously we oldsters must have been doing something wrong. In July we were enthroned on the seats of power; by January we had built an empty society that could only be redeemed by the "Now Generation," as *Time* labeled our successors— the boys and girls under twenty-five who "have already staked out their own mini-society, a congruent culture," and who would "write finis to poverty and war." Though "psephologists call them 'alien-

ated,'" they have a "hunger for sentience," *Time* pointed out. "In the omphalocentric process of self-construction and discovery, [the Man of the Year] stalks love like a wary hunter, but has no time or target."

Frankly, friends, that kind of writing gives me a pain in the omphalos. But it is not because I begrudge the Now Generation its swift return to the spotlight. Probably we of the deposed Command Generation didn't deserve more than the twenty-three weeks that our reign lasted, and if today's kids can write finis to poverty and war, and infuse the future with a transcendent ethic, they should be given every chance.

What I do begrudge is that there's no hiding place down here for any of us, old or young, from journalism's relentless classifiers. We are typed and stereotyped with our age bracket, and only a few gaps remain for a person who would just like to be himself. As things stand, the Command Generation embraces everyone from forty to sixty and merges into the Medicare Generation. The Now Generation ends at twenty-five and reaches back to fifteen.

Now you might think that this leaves plenty of room in the middle—from twenty-six to thirty-nine—for anyone who wants to squirm out of his assigned category. But it isn't that easy. What about the Silent Generation? I'll bet you forgot all about them. That's because they're so silent. They were silent back in the Korean War days, and they still are, but that doesn't mean they aren't *there*. They're packed solid from thirty-two to thirty-nine.

Well then, you say, that leaves twenty-six to thirty-one. Don't be so sure. How about the Beat Generation? They're in there, too —right behind Silent and ahead of Now, massed in full strength at thirty-one and tapering off at twenty-seven. That leaves twenty-six. If you want to be an individual in America today, my advice is to grab twenty-six. The only other choice is to drop back among the teeny-boppers, but who wants to be fourteen again? Not me. I'm having too much fun drinking up the golden decades like nectar at the banquet table of life.

By WILLIAM K. ZINSSER